Kaizen

The Japanese Method
for Transforming Habits,
One Small Step at a Time

SARAH HARVEY

bluebird
books for life

First published 2019 by Bluebird
an imprint of Pan Macmillan
20 New Wharf Road, London N1 9RR
Associated companies throughout the world
www.panmacmillan.com

ISBN 978-1-5290-0535-6

1 3 5 7 9 8 6 4 2

A CIP catalogue record for this book is available from the British Library.

Designed by Justine Anweiler
Illustrated by Mel Four
Printed and bound in China

Visit www.bluebird.com to read more about all our books
and to buy them. You will also find features, author interviews and
news of any author events, and you can sign up for e-newsletters
so that you're always first to hear about our new releases.

CONTENTS

Prologue: Kaizen & Me 6

Introduction 12

How to Start 37

Health 59

Work 119

Money 163

Home 183

Relationships 207

Habits & Challenges 227

Stumbling Blocks 257

Conclusion: Change for Good 264

About the Author 267

Acknowledgements, Endnotes
& Picture Credits 268

PROLOGUE

KAIZEN AND ME

In September 2017, I decided to quit my job working for a London publisher and move to Japan. I enjoyed my job and had a fun social life but was feeling burnt out and anxious. The political landscape was uncertain, and I was feeling increasingly out of control. I tried to do yoga and practise mindfulness as much as possible, but I found that it wasn't enough to combat the feelings of anxiety and instability I had about the future. I wanted to change some of my behaviours that I knew weren't doing me any good but I found it difficult to keep up with any new habits. In short: I was tired, creatively uninspired and definitely needed a break from my routine.

As soon as I moved to Japan I noticed how, even when you were in a busy or built-up place, there was a sense of calm. The Tokyo Metro at rush hour was just as populated – if not more so – than the London Underground, but there would be no passive-aggressive jostling for space. You would be packed into carriages like sardines but it would be practically silent. The traffic was almost exclusively congested but nobody would beep their horns or drive erratically. You hardly ever saw anybody rushing; there was a sense of order and a slower pace. My new Japanese home was bigger and busier in places, but somehow less frantic and a far more welcoming, clean and relaxing space to be in. And from that, I felt encouraged to slow down, make some lifestyle changes and embrace new, more enriching and creative challenges. Taking a step into a different culture showed me some of the things I was getting wrong with my habits and routine in London, where I often rushed around on autopilot, and wasn't always looking after myself in the best way.

After living in Japan for six months and noticing these differences in my own behaviour, I became fascinated by how small details and incremental change were given more emphasis in Japanese daily life. If you saw a road being resurfaced, there would be a huge team working on it, each focusing on a very small task, whether that was measuring out the space, doing the digging or directing pedestrians around the footpath. Rather than the job taking weeks (or years!), the entire road would be back in action within a few days. I learned of sushi chefs who train for seven whole years, each part of the process taught meticulously. In my Japanese lessons, I was taught how important it is that the strokes of the Japanese script are performed in a certain order – the *kakijun* – and that it takes children almost the entirety of their compulsory education to learn the full set of 2,136 kanji characters. Small details matter in Japanese culture. I started researching this aspect of Japanese life and, through this, I discovered the philosophy and practice of Kaizen (Ky'zen).

Roughly translating from Japanese into 'good change' or 'improvement', the philosophy of Kaizen isn't about change for change's sake, but about identifying particular goals – both short-term and long-term – and then making small, manageable steps to achieve those goals. Rather than forcing us to make big dramatic changes, the method emphasizes doing things incrementally.

Kaizen uses the psychological teaching around why we find it hard to give up bad habits and stick to new challenges, and offers a clear structural framework for going about change. It is most commonly

known as a business methodology, but it has clear benefits for your own personal development too. It can transform the way that you feel about yourself, your goals and your environment.

Learning about Kaizen made me think about the long history that we have of looking to others – particularly in the East – for wisdom about living well and with happiness. We are living in uncertain and stressful times and I don't think it is any coincidence that this has resulted in a recent flurry of interest in looking to other cultures and traditions for guidance. This can be seen in the trends for all things Scandinavian – whether that is *hygge, lagom, lykke* or *sisu* – or Japanese concepts, such as *ikigai, wabi-sabi, kakeibo, kintsugi, shinrin-yoku,* and Marie Kondo's popular decluttering methods.

Having a change of scene and introducing new experiences into my life meant that I found it easier to break away from my previous routine. I started to take on some new, positive habits in the spirit of Kaizen. I felt inspired to write again and started doing morning yoga every day, an activity I had previously enjoyed but which I had allowed to lapse. Some of my habits changed through no choice of my own (it is very hard to find decent Cheddar cheese to gorge on in Tokyo!) but I also started to change things of my own volition. Being away from my usual temptations and triggers shone a light on where I was misstepping before, in both my personal and working life. I was now working as a freelancer and this illuminated many of the things that I had been getting wrong with my previous office-based working life. It also meant that I suddenly had to learn to be disciplined with time and not let work bleed into my evenings too much (although I often failed with this, I have to be honest!).

I am now back in London and there are a number of small changes I made during my time in Japan that have become fundamental to my daily life. I am more mindful of how my actions impact upon my physical and mental health, particularly how I need to slow down, say 'no' to invitations, and take breaks from social media and the relentless news cycle. Japanese society is by no means a perfect one – Japan's gender gap was ranked at a miserable 114th out of

144 countries in 2017[1]: by far the worst of the top seven major economies. It also has some of the longest working hours in the developed world, with a systemic culture of overtime.[2] But using my time in Japan as an opportunity to reflect, taking a step back from habits that had become second nature, and learning from another culture has made me think closely about the ways in which I was behaving before. It has transformed the way I go about my daily life. I feel far more creative, relaxed and focused.

Kaizen is useful for anybody wishing to change their routine. Rather than making any scary leaps into the dark, it is about stepping back and analysing your current habits, deciding what you could improve in your existing life, or thinking of new challenges you could start, then putting into place a plan to change in very small incremental stages. You will hardly even notice the difference to your routine. There are countless books that promise solutions to a happy life – various daft fasting diets, 'eat clean' people telling us to eat more coconut oil, and extreme exercise routines from nutty-chested former army cadets with twelve packs. Most people find that these solutions are far too extreme, their busy lives get in the way, and they find it a struggle to sustain these kinds of changes in the long term. Having consulted a number of psychologists who specialize in habitual behaviour, the consensus is that making incremental changes to your habits is the key to sustainable results.

My life is by no means flawless; I don't own a beautiful mansion overlooking a lake, and there are days where I realize I have only eaten beige food. But I am definitely becoming more mindful of my behaviour and habits, and slowly improving the areas of my life where I felt dissatisfied before. I am looking after myself better and feel more inspired to learn and achieve new things. Amending my behaviour with small actions has been transformative. And as my friends and family would attest, if I can do it, then you can too! I have consulted Kaizen practitioners, psychologists and inspiring people from my own life so that, over the following chapters, I can show how incremental change can have a huge transformative effect on you too.

Not many people will have the luxury of being able to up sticks and move to an entirely new continent like I did, but I would love for this book to be your passport to improving your life, even in just a few small ways, and adopting new and exciting challenges.

Sarah

INTRODUCTION

The journey of a thousand miles begins with a single step – Lao Tzu

HOW CAN THIS BOOK HELP YOU?

Welcome to the Wonderful World of Kaizen. This is usually the part where the author makes bold claims about how their book is going to instantly transform your life. This isn't to say that this book *won't* transform your life – it very much has the potential to do so – but I'm afraid that it won't do it by itself. It will, however, tool you up with useful tips and advice on how to interrogate your existing behaviour, help you understand why you abandon certain new habits or lose motivation halfway through, look at how to break free from bad habits, teach you how to keep track of your progress, and remind you to practise self-compassion along the way.

The quote from the ancient Chinese philosopher, Lao Tzu, is one often used in self-help books and on motivational screensavers, but it is one that is popular for a reason and perfectly encapsulates the Kaizen philosophy: you can change your life by making lots of small steps (and I won't force you to walk a thousand miles either).

THIS BOOK IS FOR:

⊙ Anybody who is interested in Japan or, more broadly, Eastern philosophies
⊙ Anybody who has tried to take up a new habit or behaviour in the past but struggled to keep going when life got in the way
⊙ Anybody looking to refine or change their existing behaviours

- Anybody who senses that they could be improving a certain aspect of their life but isn't sure where to start
- Anybody who has found that other 'self-help' techniques haven't worked for them and is looking for a method that they can mould to their own preferences and behaviours, playing to their strengths and minimizing their weaknesses

You can tailor Kaizen to your own needs; you can choose to do it at your own pace and work towards your own goals – not anybody else's. In doing so, you have the potential to overhaul your current habits, acquire new skills and knowledge, and abandon unproductive behaviours.

13

THE ROOTS OF KAIZEN

Kaizen is a noun in Japanese and is used to mean improvement, whether that is big or small, one-time or continuous. It is also sometimes used in relation to martial arts, where the idea of improving one area of your practice meticulously and slowly is encouraged. You are prompted to focus on one thing at a time, simply, and to practise until you get results. You could see the philosophy of Kaizen as very much 'East-meets-West' in that the business theory was actually conceived by the US government, but then brought over and used to great effect in post-World War II Japan, where the economy had been completely destroyed by the war effort. Kaizen is credited with influencing the huge success of Japanese companies in the second half of the twentieth century and has since been popularized around the world as an effective method for improving existing habits and achieving success in a number of different fields, from healthcare to psychotherapy to government institutions.

A lot of other Japanese terms that have been adopted in the West – *ikigai, wabi-sabi, shinrin yoku* – can be hard to translate directly, but the beauty of Kaizen as an improvement philosophy is that it has developed organically as a theory between the West and East. Consequently, Kaizen is not too difficult to grasp or apply to your own life. Little has been written about how an individual can apply the principles of Kaizen to aspects of their own life to bring about their own 'good change', but it is easy to adopt Kaizen and bring about lasting change in multiple areas of your life; from obvious things which people often try to improve, such as their health and finances, to inspiring more unusual change – whether that is learning how to speak Thai or becoming an expert at life drawing. It is a flexible and easily adaptable approach to change. Rather than being dictated to by a fitness guru with unobtainable abs or a hypnotist who fails to make you stop smoking in five days, Kaizen encourages you to formulate your own goals and work towards them at your own pace. You make it work for you.

> *The Kaizen philosophy assumes that our way of life – be it our working life, our social life, or our home life – deserves to be constantly improved.*[3]
> – Mr Masaaki Imai

THE HISTORY OF KAIZEN

The idea of continuous improvement was first trialled in the States during the Second World War, when it was found that businesses were struggling to innovate and keep up with supplies for the war effort when so many men were abroad fighting the war. As such, the US government created a series of programmes called Training Within Industries (TWI), which aimed to stimulate business. The emphasis was put on the existing workforce to pay attention to working practices and suggest methods for improvement themselves, rather than waiting to be dictated to from above. These programmes were judged a huge success and ensured that businesses could supply reliable equipment to the men abroad, while also keeping the domestic side of things afloat.[4]

When the war was over, a lot of these American businesses found that they had been bolstered by the war effort and no longer needed to rely on the programmes for continuous improvement. Japan, on the other hand, was completely on its knees from the loss of life at the end of the war. Its industries were decimated and morale was low. The US – interested in strengthening Japan so that it could act as a buffer to North Korea – sent over a team of advisors, led by a William Edwards Deming, to provide management training courses to Japanese businesses.[5]

The Japanese were immediately enthralled with this new management technique of continuous improvement and christened it Kaizen, the already common noun in Japanese used to mean 'good change' or 'improvement'. Businesses took to Kaizen with gusto and it was credited with helping the huge growth of the Japanese economy and the success of its businesses in the second half of the twentieth century. Most famously it was used by Toyota to improve its production line, labelled 'the Toyota Way'. The emphasis was on finding 'lean' processes, reducing production waste (or *muda*), increasing the quality of products, and encouraging workers to make suggestions as to how practices could be improved.

Rather ironically, by the 1980s, American businesses had become nervous about Japanese companies competing with them, so Kaizen returned to the US as an organizational theory.[6] It was popularized in the West by Mr Masaaki Imai, a Japanese business consultant and organizational theorist, whose teachings are still very much used by businesses around the world today.

KAIZEN AS AN ORGANIZATIONAL THEORY

Mr Masaaki Imai first popularized the theory of Kaizen in his book *Kaizen: The Key to Japan's Competitive Success*. In the book, he describes the differences he has seen between Japanese and Western working practices and from this advocates the idea that Kaizen is an extension of the Japanese value system and its incremental attitude towards change: 'I came to the conclusion that the key difference between how change is understood in Japan and how it is viewed in the West lies in the Kaizen concept – a concept that is so natural and obvious to many Japanese managers that they often do not even realize that they possess it!'[7]

Mr Imai noted how gradual change was a less obvious part of the Western way of life than it was in Japan, and that Western businesses were less successful because they always sought abrupt and dramatic change over incremental change.

It is now more than thirty years since the release of Mr Imai's book and his Kaizen Institute continues to consult for and train businesses in the philosophy of Kaizen. At first, they worked exclusively with car companies, but the Institute has since expanded across the world. They now work with lots of other sectors, from banking to retail to government organizations. Mr Imai's colleague Euclides A. Coimbra, Senior Partner and Managing Director of the Kaizen Institute Western Europe, spoke to me about the Institute and how the theory of Kaizen can be applied to individual change as well as organizational change.

In his book, Mr Imai stresses that Kaizen should be applied to every part of an organization, and Coimbra advocates this universal approach to change: 'we [the Kaizen Institute] believe that the only way to have a "Continuous Improvement Culture" is to practise improvements engaging everybody, everywhere and every day.' Continuous improvement involves everyone, whether you are a junior worker or a senior manager.

The workers at the top of the organization are encouraged to come up with short-, medium- and long-term goals for the business around four criteria: growth (or sales), quality, level of service and motivation. Every employee – whether that is the person on the reception desk, a till worker, or the foreman on the factory floor – is invited to also make suggestions on how to improve. The employees make suggestions in groups and as individuals, and the emphasis is on very small things that would transform their working process.

At the time of Imai's book release, Japanese workers each made nineteen suggestions per year on average for ways in which their companies could improve, and this level of engagement is still very much encouraged today. Success for the company is judged on whether it is more productive, more competitive and more profitable. But the emphasis is on long-term incremental improvements rather than quick and drastic change.

KAIZEN FOR PERSONAL DEVELOPMENT

Kaizen techniques can work outside of organizational theory, and Mr Imai himself acknowledges that the philosophy has wider applications than just the business world, particularly as – in his view – all individuals have an instinctive desire to improve themselves. Coimbra asserts that at the Kaizen Institute they very much encourage that: 'since we started the Kaizen Institute we have been applying what we preach internally. We have a course for our employees where we teach Kaizen principles and tools for personal development.' This optional course encourages participants to assess their lives against a number of criteria (physical, emotional, mental and spiritual) and to make suggestions for changes. Participants work on a plan involving small actions they can make to bring about improvement. This eventually becomes a 'Life Strategy', in which they are asked to summarize the changes that they are going to make on an A3 piece of paper – which mirrors the same strategy document that businesses such as Toyota use when they are formulating their Kaizen strategy.

Coimbra says that when people start their own Kaizen practice, most of the habits they are looking to change are physical, such as exercise, sleep and diet. But once employees try new habits, they are encouraged to work towards more emotional aspects of improvement. Coimbra states that 'it is common to see people adopting meditation habits and being more conscious of their own emotions and the impact they may have in the emotions of other people'. The employees who have signed up to the programme have noticed considerable improvements in their habits and happiness, including 'better exercise habits, rest and nutrition' and have demonstrated 'more sophisticated behaviours related to emotional intelligence and spiritual engagement in life as a whole'. Coimbra asserts 'our most motivated employees have the Kaizen mindset in their personal life and this of course benefits all aspects of their life'.

Change is infectious and when success is achieved in one area, you are encouraged to apply the same techniques to another area of your life. This is referred to as *yokoten* or 'horizontal deployment', i.e. copying what works in one area to see if it works in another.

The philosophy of Kaizen is just as easy to apply to individual change as to change in a business; it is about setting long-term, medium-term and short-term goals, then thinking of small, incremental adjustments you can make to work towards these goals. Coimbra argues that if you adopt the philosophy of continuous improvement 'you will always be looking for ways to do better, even if it is only improving small things on a daily basis. We can see that the long-term evolution of our society as human beings is one of continuous progress and that if we create a spiral [streak] of continuous wins we will be much better in all senses'.

Over the course of this book, as well as introducing you to Kaizen techniques and offering tips for small steps you can make to change your environment and routine in a number of areas, I will encourage you adopt this philosophy of continuous improvement. Through taking a step back and analysing your life as a whole, I hope that it will help you to see it from a different perspective; whether that's choosing to embrace nature, eating more mindfully or thinking about your career goals. And once one small change makes a difference, it is likely that you will practise your own *yokoten* and be encouraged to try another change.

KAIZEN AND SPORT

The field of sport is another area in which Kaizen techniques have already been used successfully. As well as it being used in martial arts training, several top sports teams have cited Kaizen – or 'marginal gains' as it is sometimes referred to – as a technique that they have used to great effect. Sir Dave Brailsford became head of the British cycling team in 2002, when the existing team had experienced little to no success. But by the Beijing Olympics in 2008, the team won seven of the ten possible gold medals for cycling, and achieved the same tally at the London Olympics in 2012.

Brailsford – who had an MBA and an interest in business management techniques – started to use Kaizen as a way to improve the team's performance. He got the team to break down every aspect of cycling into as small a part as possible – whether that was the aerodynamics, the nutrition of the cyclists, the maintenance of the bikes – and then gave them a target of improving each part by just 1 per cent. Rather than focusing on perfection from the start, he looked for marginal gains in each area and celebrated small successes, which soon became cumulative successes. He cites these marginal gains as creating a contagious enthusiasm for change, which then spurred the team on to even more success.[8] Brailsford is now taking his techniques to members of the British government to show how they can be applied to public services – such as Britain's National Health Service – to improve targets and overall performance.

JAPAN AND THE WEST

As we have already discussed, the continuous improvement philosophy of Kaizen is very much 'East-meets-West'. It was conceived as a business strategy in the West but was then adopted by Japanese companies, who saw the techniques as an extension of Japanese values and attitudes towards incremental change. During the course of this book I am going to explore how Kaizen is a good example of this ongoing dialogue between Japan and the West, and touch upon what we can learn from some of the other Japanese social, cultural and philosophical traditions too.

Japanese society is not without its flaws, but I think we can gain a lot from observing the way it works. One of the things that I immediately noticed when arriving in Japan is how it has retained its own sense of identity and strong social structures. You are instantly struck by small children playing out in the street unaccompanied, people leaving their bikes unlocked outside their houses and often leaving the doors to their homes unlocked, too. As a woman, it feels a lot safer to walk around at night compared to other big cities like London, Paris or New York. There are hardly any litter bins in central Tokyo (apparently because of anti-terrorism measures), but somehow no litter whatsoever – people take responsibility and carry it home with them.

There is a really strong social contract and it is so refreshing and inspirational to experience firsthand. Being more conscious of the needs of others around you and of your impact on your environment is something I feel we need to introduce into our lives as much as possible. Japan is dominated by a collectivist culture unlike any that we have in the West. It will take a foreigner a prolonged period of being immersed in Japanese culture to fully appreciate the amount of social rules and small daily courtesies that dominate the way that the Japanese interact with each other. The social structures are set up very distinctively and founded on rules that can sometimes seem alien to those outside of Japan. Because the inhabitable parts of the country are so densely populated, there has to be a big emphasis on social cohesion.

One of the most unique aspects of Japanese culture is the concept of *Uchi-Soto*, which dictates a lot of Japan's social customs and even extends to their language. Translating as *Uchi* (home/inside) and *Soto* (outside), it is about separating in-groups from out-groups. A Japanese person's in-group would be their family, close friends, and co-workers, whereas the out-group would be any clients, customers, visitors or *gaijin* (non-Japanese people). When speaking with someone from an out-group, the out-group must be 'honoured', and the in-group 'humbled', which means that different language is used to convey a level of politeness depending on who you are talking to. This also extends to gift-giving and other social interactions such as serving, where the customer is treated with the ultimate respect. The upside of this is the strong social contract and relative social cohesion between Japanese people and the respect and politeness that an outsider will feel when visiting Japan. The downside of these rules is that as an outsider it can be hard to be fully accepted

in Japanese society; for example, my British friend has been living in Tokyo for fifteen years, is fluent in Japanese and has a Japanese wife, but still feels like he isn't fully integrated into society. Younger people are said to be embracing these rules less, but they are still fundamental to Japanese society and business culture.

Although there are many things in Japan that a naive westerner will recognize – there are American coffee shops on every corner, Western-style sit-down toilets favoured over traditional squat toilets and gigantic Scandinavian fashion stores seemingly everywhere – a short time there will make you realize that, as well as there being traditional social structures, there is also still a huge emphasis on traditional Japanese craft and design. There is a definite melding of Western culture with traditional Japanese culture. You will see teenage girls dressed up in traditional kimonos, or the lighter versions, yukata, in summer, but their mates might be wearing the latest Nike trainers or a new cult skater brand. This mixing of cultures also happens in the home. I visited and lived in a number of different homes during my time in Japan and some of them were super-modern apartments with Western-style beds and sofas, while others still had futons to sleep on and retained the traditional design of tatami matting on the floor. The choice of bedding would often fit the practicalities of the space, with traditional bedding often used in smaller apartments, so that it can be folded up out of the way during the day.

Many attribute Japan's distinctive social structures and emphasis on simple, beautiful design to the fact that the country was isolated for 220 years until the Meiji-era 'open door policy' in 1868. Prior to that, Japan was a Sakoku (closed country) with an isolationist foreign policy. Trade between Japan and other countries was severely limited, Japanese people were stopped from leaving the country, and almost all foreigners were barred from entry. There was some very limited trade with other countries, and some Western inventions were introduced into Japan this way, mostly via its trade with the Dutch East India Company; but, on the whole, exposure to the rest of the world for everyday Japanese people was non-existent. This meant that Japan's social structures, design and culture were allowed to flourish without any external influences.

When Japan was opened up again, there was a huge flurry of interest from the West in Japanese society and culture, and a desire to influence it themselves. The Meiji Restoration Period of 1868–1912 saw the dismantling of the previous governmental structures of the Edo Period of 1603–1867, where Japan had been ruled by the Tokugawa Shogunate, a feudal military-style government. The Meiji Period saw the establishment of a representative democracy, the foundation of the Tokyo police force based on the model used in Paris, and the introduction of Western cultural activities, such as baseball (now one of Japan's biggest sports). Japanese ideas also flowed back the other way, with the French art critic Philippe Burty coining the term *Japonisme* in the early 1870s to describe the massive appetite for Japanese design and art in both France and elsewhere. This can be seen in the painting, sculpture and architecture of Europe in the late nineteenth century, particularly the impressionist artists, the aesthetic movement and art nouveau.[9]

This opening-up of Japan in the nineteenth century started a dialogue with the rest of the world that has been continuing ever since, and it is a dialogue which has often been contentious. The American Occupation of Japan between 1945 and 1952 introduced reforms that are still in place today, such as the suffrage of women and a new co-education system, but it also sped up the influence that the West was having upon Japanese society. Some have argued that the Sakoku period of isolation firmly cemented certain values and traditions that make Japan unique, but that these have been continuously under threat from the onslaught of foreign influence ever since.

The dialogue between Japan and the West continues to develop and ebb and flow, and the philosophy of Kaizen can be seen as this dialogue in action. It is an idea which came to Japan from the West, but was very much aligned with the traditional Japanese attitude towards gradual change, before being eventually exported back to the West.

WHY IS KAIZEN USEFUL NOW?

There are a lot of problems in the world that are out of our control. But for the parts of our lives over which we can have more control, Kaizen is a great way to reduce sources of stress and bring about new, exciting improvements. While inept politicians and worries about climate change aren't going anywhere (unfortunately), Kaizen can be used to bring more harmony into your immediate environment and improve your wellbeing, so that you have more energy to face and fight the problems of the wider world.

Unlike expensive gym memberships that go unused or an impulse purchase which you have forgotten about by the next day, Kaizen is free and accessible to anyone; the only thing you really need to start is a pen and paper to draw up your initial plan and track your goals.

The emphasis is on making small, incremental changes to parts of your routine, which can easily fit around work, childcare or social commitments. The changes should be so small that at first you barely notice any difference to your daily life. As the British cycling team looked to improve aspects of their process by just 1 per cent, this is the amount of impact upon your routine you should be looking at too. It is adding one more fruit or vegetable item to your food shop or meditating for five minutes every Saturday morning. Once you have made one change to a habit or formed a new one, then you can decide if you wish to step up that habit or move on to changing or obtaining a different one, for example if you have meditated every Saturday for a month and found it beneficial, then you could start including more days in your routine or meditating for slightly longer. You should find that this small feeling of success is contagious and will spur you on to achieve even more.

WHY DO WE HAVE HABITS?

Ben Gardner, Senior Lecturer in Psychology at King's College London, offers a perspective on habitual behaviour from the world of psychology. Explaining that habitual behaviours are essential to be able to function every day, Gardner tells me that we develop habitual patterns because it is our brain's way of locking in useful responses. He describes people as 'cognitive misers', i.e. we like (and need) to conserve our mental resources so that we can then use those resources on other, more mindful tasks. He gives an example:

> 'If we develop a habit for, for example, putting a teabag in a cup after taking the cup from the cupboard, then that becomes one less thing that we need to think about. So then, our tea-making does not require us to deliberate over the next steps ("I've taken the cup out of the cupboard – what next?"), but instead can proceed on autopilot, allowing us the mental space to think about other things (for example, trying to solve a work-related problem while making tea).'

It is important to state that not all habits are inherently negative, as they are essential for us to be able to function on an everyday level. If we had to pay close attention to every single task that we undertake – such as walking up some stairs or drinking a sip of water – we would be constantly exhausted. What this can mean, however, is that we also turn to our bad habits for comfort and safety when we are feeling low or tired. For example, if I have had a tough day at work, I always have a strong desire to go shopping or order an unhealthy takeaway. Escaping from the safety zone of our habitual behaviours can be difficult and, as a result, it can mean that we go about a lot of our life on autopilot or acting in ways that we know aren't good for us.

With many little strokes a large tree is felled – Japanese proverb

WHY IS IT SO HARD TO CHANGE OUR HABITS?

Habits are seductive and save us a lot of time and energy, so when it then comes to changing them it can seem a scary and daunting prospect. Gardner agrees:

'The downside of our brains "locking in" behaviours becomes clear when we want to change those behaviours. Habitual behaviours can proceed even when we lack the motivation to do them – and sometimes, when we expressly do NOT want to do them. This can be useful where they "help us over the line" with good behaviours; for example, if I have formed a habit of going for a run each morning when I wake up, and one morning I wake up and feel demotivated, my habit is going to help me to ensure I go anyway, despite my lack of motivation. The flipside of this is that, if we have "locked in" something like smoking (as an automatic response to, for example, waking up, or experiencing stress), then that behaviour becomes very hard to change via motivational means. In other words, you may successfully change a smoker's motivation, educating them of the dangers of smoking, but if they smoke habitually, despite being motivated not to do so, then changing their motivation won't translate into changing their behaviour.'

One initial step towards understanding how to change our habitual behaviours is to educate ourselves as to how we acquire habitual behaviours in the first place:

'We learn habits through repeated and rewarding performances in the presence of cues; for example, if we repeatedly bite our nails (behaviour) when we are in stressful situations (cue), and we find nail-biting to help us to deal with stress (reward), then we develop an association between stress and nail-biting. Each time we repeat the nail-biting in response to the stress cue, so that association strengthens, to the point beyond which merely encountering the stress cue is sufficient to prompt us to enact the associated behaviour automatically, without thinking about it'.

So, in order to try to tackle the underlying habits, we have to identify what our cues are for the unwanted behaviours, for example work stress is a cue for me to want to go shopping.

As well as being aware of the cues for certain habits, we should also be conscious of the (often temporary) rewards that we gain from the behaviour and how these rewards can influence our desire to repeat the behaviour in the future. Gardner asserts that the positive (even if short-lived) way these rewards make us feel, makes getting people to change their behaviour more difficult than simply educating them on the dangers of certain 'bad' behaviours. The reason for this is because some 'good' behaviours simply aren't rewarding enough for us. Gardner says:

'We don't experience such big and rapid rewards from doing [good behaviours] as we do from some bad behaviours. The motivational system is chaotic; at any one moment, there are multiple potential wants and needs that compete to push and pull us this way and that. Often, competing desires arise at the moment when we plan to "be good". It is always tempting to take the more immediately gratifying option (smoke the cigarette) than the more long-term reward (don't smoke the cigarette) . . . For those behaviours that deliver greater rewards, or more immediate rewards, it is likely to be more difficult to change these habits.'

EMOTIONS AND CHANGING HABITS

Everybody has a friend who seems to boldly go from achieving one big goal to the next without seeming to break a sweat. They suddenly decide to quit smoking one day and never touch a cigarette again, or they announce that they are going to do a triathlon and easily complete it without even seeming to train (or moan). There are some personality types that embrace dramatic change and can easily achieve their goals, seemingly without any self-doubt or hiccups. Let's face it: if you're not one of them, these people are incredibly annoying!

But if you do struggle with change, or frequently give up on New Year's resolutions two weeks into January, then you are absolutely not alone. This is because the brain is programmed to react to change in a certain way. Change can be emotionally triggering, and it is a very human response to fear and resist anything that takes you out of your comfort zone, even if you know deep down that the change would benefit you. This is especially difficult if you experience a strong – if temporary – reward from carrying out the behaviour.

Recent psychological studies[10] have concluded that the reason that some people find it easier to control their actions and resist temptation to perform bad habits than others isn't because they have greater willpower; it is because they have found a way to make it easier to form new habits and automate their behaviour to get them to their goals. The good news is that anybody can train themselves to do this – and Kaizen provides the perfect framework with which to do so.

HOW LONG DOES CHANGE TAKE?

The statistic that is often bandied about in articles about changing your behaviour is that it takes twenty-one days to form a habit. A study by psychologists at UCL has shown this number to be entirely fictitious, however.[11] Their findings in fact show that the amount of time that people take to reach 'automaticity' with their habits (performing them with efficiency, lack of awareness and/ or unintentionally) can be anything between 18 and 254 days. The length of time to reaching automaticity varies greatly depending on the person and the habit, and there have not been enough studies done for any definitive conclusions to be drawn.

There is consensus, however, that if you want to transform your habits in the long term, the new behaviour is best acquired through *incremental* strengthening of the association between the situation in which the habit is performed (for example, when/where in your daily routine you do the action) and the action itself. The more that you repeat a certain habit in a certain situation, the more likely you will be able to automate it. Ben Gardner believes that drastic change to your habits can work in some situations (for example, if somebody wishes to crash-diet for their wedding), but that 'the danger of the more drastic change method is that it may be less sustainable over time . . . We may experience an aborted behaviour change attempt as a failure, and failure can be off-putting, preventing us from wanting to try again'. As the Kaizen method encourages you to change your habits in a very incremental way and to be gentle on yourself if things don't go to plan, there is less chance of you experiencing these feelings of failure.

A NOTE ON NEGATIVITY BIAS

Your brain has what is termed by psychologists as a 'negativity bias', stemming from the early stages of evolution where a human's survival very much depended upon their ability to perceive danger. We respond to things of a negative nature much more strongly than we do to those of a positive nature. The amygdala (the 'alarm bell' of the brain) responds to each negative experience we have and becomes even more sensitive over time. This means that we usually overestimate threats and underestimate rewards and opportunities (such as a positive change in our habits). This served us well when we were living in caves and potentially about to be attacked by a pack of lions, but it isn't so useful when it is crippling our creativity and driving feelings of procrastination and inertia. The status quo is a very seductive thing, while starting something new or changing an existing habit is a far scarier thought.

People who can make changes to their routine easily are able to turn this feeling of fear into excitement, and you may find that there are some occasions when you, too, find that change is exciting and easy to achieve. But, on the whole, most of the time we will find the thought of change terrifying and will want to return to our secure and safe routine where there isn't the risk that we might not succeed. The good news is that negativity bias can be overcome and using Kaizen techniques to adopt a new habit or creative challenge can be an extremely effective way of combatting it.

THE INNER CRITIC

The voice of negativity bias is often termed our 'inner critic'. Our inner critic is a massive pain in the arse who frequently voices the fear that we won't succeed when we either try to change our habits or start a new challenge. This results in us either not attempting the change in the first place or us giving up shortly into a project.[12] Research from Strava, the social network for athletes, discovered that most people start to waver in their commitment to their New Year's Resolutions by 12 January![13] This is why there are huge industries built around people's inability to stick to goals, whether that is the expensive 'health food' delivery services that crop up in May and target people wanting to look good on the beach during their holidays, or the glossy gyms that try to lock you in to pricey contracts in January that you will have stopped using by March.

How to silence your inner critic

Mindfulness techniques are a great way of taking stock, connecting with our feelings and environment, and finding new ways of approaching the world. We'll draw upon these techniques later in the book, as they can be very useful in helping you to take a step back, slow down and process negative feelings.

As well as mindfulness, other psychologists such as Robert Maurer – Director of Behavioral Sciences at Santa Monica UCLA Medical Center – have specifically encouraged the use of Kaizen techniques as a way to combat our inner critic. The reason being that the Kaizen method of change is so incremental that it fails to trigger the body's fight-or-flight response system. Robert Maurer writes: 'If the amygdala is like an alarm system, small steps are like a cat burglar. Quietly, slowly, and softly, they pad past your fears. Your alarm never goes off.'[14] The beauty of making changes in small steps is that it creates new neural pathways before your fight-or-flight response or inner critic can be awakened.

KAIZEN IN PRACTICE

We have introduced the concept and methodology behind Kaizen and learned about how it can be used to rewire the brain's chemistry to make you more likely to stick to habits and new challenges. Now let's explore the practical application and focus on particular areas in which Kaizen can be transformative. The following chapters will show you how to make changes to your life by introducing Kaizen into your routine. Eventually it will feel like second nature.

how to start

●○○○○○○○

HOW TO START

Kaizen starts with a problem, or more precisely, with the recognition that a problem exists. – Mr Masaaki Imai[15]

The beauty of Kaizen is that once you have grasped the method you can apply it to pretty much any part of your life. It is a flexible and personalized approach to change, so everybody will have their own experience.

To help you along the way, I have included chapters on some of the most important areas of life and the habits that people often feel they want to change. Within these chapters, I have also explored other popular Japanese concepts that can be used to transform your habits or reframe the way that you think about your life. Each of these chapters also includes tips and exercises for very small steps to help you kickstart your Kaizen practices. The chosen topics are by no means exhaustive, however, so do feel free to apply the method to another part of your life which you would like to transform.

If you are struggling to keep going with your goals, skip to a chapter called Stumbling Blocks (pages 256–263) with tips to help you return to your Kaizen practice. The idea behind Kaizen is to make changes so incrementally that it is actually difficult to give up entirely.

Its continuous nature also means that there is no specific endpoint
and you are encouraged to keep finding new challenges. But life can
throw curveballs and make it difficult to sustain good habits at times,
so do be gentle on yourself if things don't always go quite to plan.

THE METHOD

Now it is time to actually bring in the method and put together a
plan. The emphasis in Kaizen is always on doing things in small
stages and treating the idea of change as an ongoing process rather
than a quick-fix 'to-do list'.

The method will show you how to interrogate your existing habits,
think about long-term goals, and then formulate a plan to start
gradually making small improvements towards those goals. In
the process, you will overhaul your mindset and attitude towards
change. The most important thing to ensure you stay motivated is
that the small changes shouldn't feel too scary or impact upon your
existing routine too much.

Because each person will have different priorities and things they
wish to transform, the method isn't prescriptive or one-size-fits-all.
Various Kaizen practitioners work in different ways and no person's
plan is going to look the same. But there are certain questions
we can all start with to stimulate your thinking and provoke
thoughtful responses.

THE INVENTORY

Let's start by taking an inventory of your life as it is at this very moment. The idea is to make an honest assessment of your habits and immediate environment to eventually form a 'life plan' of goals and challenges. This probably sounds like a daunting task, so let's adopt a Kaizen attitude and break it down into small steps.

Take out a piece of paper and divide it into sections. This can either be in columns or a spider diagram, whichever is more aesthetically pleasing to you. Nobody has to see this so do whatever feels right for you. If it feels too daunting to try to tackle every part of your life at once, just choose one or two things to concentrate on at a time. Each person will have different priorities and you can populate this inventory with anything you like, but here are some ideas:

Health – What is your relationship with: your body, your mental health, diet, exercise routine (or lack of), sleep patterns? Which areas are you happy with and where is there room for improvement?

Working life/career – Are you happy in your job? Are you looking for work or a career change? Do you feel fulfilled in your working life? How do you get on with your colleagues? A key thing to address here might be work–life balance. If you are working towards a qualification, are you happy with the way that you study? Do you maximize your time effectively? Or are you currently stuck in a boring job and contemplating going back to study?

Money – Do an honest assessment of your attitude towards money and your current financial status. Do you have debt that you wish you could clear? Or is there something that you would like to save up for? Do you find that you have an emotional attitude to spending or are you fully in control?

Home – How do you feel about your immediate environment and the people in it? Are you happy or are there things you would like to change?

Relationships – How do you feel about your partner, your friends and members of your family? What are the relationships that boost you? Are there any relationships that drain you or ones that could be improved?

New challenges – What new challenges could you set yourself? Have you always wanted to learn a language or an instrument, master a certain cuisine or try a new sport? Try to think of a few positive goals that you could work towards.

This is a lot to take in, so at first try taking just one or two areas and brainstorming those. You can come to the others later. There will probably be some areas which immediately spring to mind in terms of where you would like to see change. You could be struggling to stay on a diet, or you could feel stuck in a job that you hate but feel too overwhelmed to look for another one. Although the big things that leap out will be your priority, do not neglect small things in the same area that could also be important and are potentially the 'quick wins' to improving your life.

As well as including the existing areas of your life that you want to change, think about potential new challenges too. Rather than only listing things you are currently unhappy about, try to include some new and exciting possibilities as well. It will be more motivating (and less miserable!) if your inventory includes a mixture of old behaviours that you wish to change and new activities you might want to try.

THINGS YOU WANT TO CHANGE

Let's focus on your existing habits first. Now is the time to look at your inventory and really interrogate yourself. Take out a new piece of paper, and for each area be brutally honest and question whether you are happy and doing the most to achieve what you want. For the areas you want to change, think about what could be done to improve your situation. Here are some questions to help:

> *How am I successful in this area?*
> *How could I do better or how am I ineffectual?*
> *What would it look like if I had a much-improved situation?*
> *What are some very small short-term steps I can take*
> *to get started towards this much-improved situation?*
> *What would long-term success look like?*

Take your time over these questions, as the answers to them might not be immediately obvious. Perhaps take a different area each day and put together your answers over the course of a week. Your subconscious brain loves working on questions in the background and you might suddenly find that an answer comes to you when you're in the shower or queuing for a sandwich at lunchtime.

FOR EXAMPLE

Home: Living in a house-share

How am I successful in this area?

I have found housemates whom I like (when they aren't leaving the toilet seat up/failing to empty the dishwasher/having impromptu house parties on Monday nights. . .).

How could I do better?

I could be more honest with my housemates about my grievances with living in a shared house rather than stew about them in private in my room.

What would it look like if I had a much-improved situation?

I would love to come home to a stress-free environment.

What are some very small short-term steps I can take to get started towards this much-improved situation?

I could talk to one of my housemates about how I feel.

What would long-term success look like?

A more harmonious living situation.

It is illuminating to spend time tracking existing habits to see where you might be able to improve, for example keeping a food/exercise diary over a week or interrogating where you spend time at work. I have included tips about keeping a journal on page 55 and there are various apps that can assist with this too, depending on the habit.

If you can identify an area that you want to improve but find it difficult to pinpoint actions that might help, the following chapters contain ideas for steps you can take in each area of your life.

> *Note: There may be existing areas of your life that you wish you could change but aren't able to because of circumstances that are out of your control. It could be that you are a carer for a family member, suffering from an illness or unable to change your job because of your location. If this is the case, try to concentrate on other things you can do to improve your quality of life or set yourself some new positive goals that you can work towards. I have tried to include as many small and inexpensive tips as possible for when it feels hard to make progress.*

From the answers that you have given to the questions opposite, you will find that you have a goal – or several goals – and a list of actions. They should be very small actions that you can take in the short term to work towards more long-term happiness and success.

If you have a set idea of a goal you want to work towards, try writing it down and keeping it somewhere where you can see it regularly, such as in your purse, on your computer screen or on a sticky note attached to your mirror.

EXAMPLES
I want to learn how to drive.
I want to reduce the balance on my credit card.
I would like to reconnect with an old school friend.

If you're still unsure about your short-, medium- and long-term goals, there are lots of tips in the following sections, so don't worry. You don't have to have your whole life planned out right away, but do keep these goals in the back of your mind when progressing through the book.

NEW CHALLENGES AND HOBBIES

For any new challenges that you wish to take on, the first step is to do a brainstorm of what these could be. Is there a hobby you used to do at school that fell by the wayside when life got in the way? Is there a country you have always dreamed of visiting that you want to save up to go to? And would you like to know some of the language before you go? Or is there a physical or mental challenge you have always fancied trying?

There are probably a few things that spring to mind straight away, but if you are struggling to think of anything then canvas friends and the internet for inspiration. Check out local Facebook groups to see if there is an activity that you can try close to home, or if you want to try something a bit more unusual then consult the many websites and online forums that provide advice on nearly every activity you can think of. There are also plenty of tips in the Habits and Challenges chapter (see pages 226–255).

Once you have decided what this challenge could be, again ask yourself some small questions about how you can get started.

> *What will the challenge involve?*
> *Why do I want to do it?*
> *What is a very small thing I can do to get started?*
> *What would long-term success look like?*

FOR EXAMPLE

What will the challenge involve?
I want to run a 10K.

Why do I want to do it?
For the physical and mental challenge.

What is a very small thing I can do to get started?
Download a running app to my phone and try out a first run.

What would long-term success look like?
Completing the challenge and raising lots of money for charity.

Having both short-term and long-term goals in mind will keep you focused on why you want to embark on such a challenge, and breaking them down into chunks will seem less overwhelming.

Using one of these new challenges to distract you from an old unwanted habit is a brilliant way to channel your mindset into something positive, for example, every time you go to scroll through Twitter, spend a minute on your language-learning app instead.

NEXT STEPS

Once you have mapped out the various areas of your life on which you wish to concentrate, it is time to prioritize. Ask yourself whether there any 'quick wins' that can be sorted out fairly easily, and, rather than overwhelm yourself at the start, perhaps choose just one area to focus on (although it is worth looking at all of your answers as a whole to see if there are any overlaps or things that could be worked on in unison, for example 'I want to move about more' and 'I want to learn Beyonce's dance routine to "Single Ladies"' could be combined as one goal).

Once you have chosen your first area of focus, now is the time to write down the *smallest thing* you can do to work towards that goal. Remember the 1 per cent rule! It should be something that will barely impact your routine and be a tiny incremental step towards your goal.

FOR EXAMPLE

Goal: Learning Beyonce's 'Single Ladies' dance routine in time for my friend's hen do.

First small step: Watch the music video and then draw up a plan of which sections you are going to learn. Rather than trying to learn the whole routine in one go, all you need to do is allocate five minutes of your day – whether that is setting your morning alarm five minutes earlier, devoting five minutes to it when you return from work or before you go to bed – and build up from there.

WHAT IS YOUR TIME FRAME?

Think about when you would like to complete your goal. This will vary depending on what you are trying to achieve – aiming to learn a musical instrument is going to take longer than reading *Ulysses* (in theory, at least!). Your goal might not have a finite ending, especially if it is a new hobby. The key is to make sure that you have a measurable time frame so that you can track progress, for example, 'I want to take up yoga, so I'll go to one class every fortnight.'

You might find that it is occupying all of your energy and making you feel exhausted. If that is the case, then perhaps make the step you are working towards *even smaller*. For example, if you are failing to write 200 words each day, then reduce it to just 100. This might not seem like very much, but finishing the week having written 700 words is better than staring at a screen while losing all motivation.

You should find that once you have started to incorporate one small new step into your routine – and things start to develop – then you will have more energy to tackle other things too. You can now either ramp up the step you are already working on or bring in an entirely new step.

HOLDING YOURSELF ACCOUNTABLE

Now that you have an idea of what you want to achieve and the first small measurable step you can do towards it, it is time to find a way to make yourself accountable. Different people will respond to different ways, but some ideas are:

Use a bullet journal. Bullet journals may sound complicated but they are really easy to put together and a great way to track your progress. There is a full guide to how to produce one on page 55. Following #bulletjournal on social media will also provide much inspiration for how to create one.

A good old-fashioned wall chart. Did you used to have a chart at home where your parents rewarded you for good behaviour or eating your greens? Or did your teacher use one to reward pupils who had been helpful in class? Make one for yourself and display it in pride of place at home. Buy colourful paper and stickers to make it look even fancier.

Tell a friend. Informing somebody else of your goal and letting them help hold you to account is a good way of spurring you on. I asked my friend to check in on my word count while I was writing this book and it really motivated me (and I only lied a few times!).

Online trackers and apps. Technology can sometimes be a very good thing, especially when it comes to analysing your habits or tracking your goals. Explore the many different options out there for apps that can offer encouragement and help you to keep track of your progress.

REWARD YOURSELF

As well as tracking your achievements, a good way to feel motivated is to reward yourself when you make progress. Reaching some of your goals will feel rewarding enough – especially if you are getting a boost in mood from better sleep or doing more exercise – but some habits may feel harder to change. And your rewards can be small, such as a new notebook or a plant for your bedroom. This can spur you on and encourage you to try to conquer even more challenges. Another idea of a way to treat yourself could be with fun cultural or social activities. For example, after finally running 5K without stopping, why don't you arrange a celebratory karaoke night or night out with your friends? Involving others in your rewards will mean that your friends can both motivate you and hold you to account if you don't stick to your goals.

JOURNALING

The very first part of the Kaizen method is about taking stock and interrogating your existing habitual behaviours. Lots of books encourage readers to 'keep a journal' to do this but don't explain how.

Bullet journaling is a technique of creating and designing your own type of journal, and, unlike the strict layout of a diary (and the guilt that you feel when you inevitably miss filling in an entry!), you are in control of the blank spaces and can use it as much or as little as you want to. It isn't something that you necessarily have to engage with every day. You can mould your journal to be the perfect tool to track both your habits and your Kaizen goals.

I now use a journal every day to track my habits and to make plans for future Kaizen challenges. Being able to look back over previous weeks and months to see how my behaviours have changed or how a new habit has become second nature is really illuminating and motivating. It also brings into focus things that I am struggling to change and need to work on.

If you aren't a journaling type, I have included lots of other tips for ways to track your habits, such as the distance that you have walked or the quality of your sleep. See what works for you. The important thing is that you track your habits; the means of getting there doesn't matter.

HOW TO START A KAIZEN JOURNAL

I recommend setting this up yourself in a notebook so that you can tailor it to what you want and need – it honestly only takes a small amount of time and you only need a few basics to get started. Use the following sections initially, then you can expand it further. Key sections could be:

Monthly calendar. I find it useful to divide my journal into months and just set up one month at a time. This means that you can adapt the next month according to what you used and found helpful in the previous month. To make a monthly calendar, write the name of the month at the top (you can make it look fancy if you wish!) then list the dates of that month in a column down the far left-hand side of the page. Fill in any important events that month.

Monthly goals. Adjacent to the calendar page, write a list of bullet points for things that you want to achieve that month. These can be anything from spending targets ('I don't want to go into my overdraft'), health goals ('I intend to go to four Pilates classes this month'), creative challenges ('I will learn the E Minor scale on the piano') or work targets ('I will organize a charity bake sale' or 'I won't stab Carlo in the head with a biro when he is rude to me').

Habit tracker. This is the section that I use to track a few habits (sleep/exercise/eating habits/spending, etc.). The layout for this will depend on what it is that you are tracking, but if it is something that I wish to track on a daily basis then I will turn the page horizontally and write the days of the month along the top (leaving a 5cm column blank on the left). I then write whatever goal or habit I have in the blank column. If I have achieved the habit on that day, then I will colour in the corresponding space or fill it in with a number if more relevant.

Gratitude list. Next to my habit tracker I like to include a gratitude list that I fill in each day (more on this in the Relationships chapter, see page 212).

Daily or weekly to-do list. I don't always use my journal every single day so don't worry if you aren't keeping up with it! But when I am using it as a daily to-do list, I write the day/date and then make a list of bullets underneath of things that I wish to achieve. Try to include a few items rather than a huge list that you will never get through! When you come to the next day, look over your previous day's list, draw a forward arrow over the bullet (key below) and move anything you didn't achieve into your new day. If the task is no longer relevant, then ignore it. Cross out things you've achieved and feel very smug.

Bullet key
- To do
- ~~Completed~~
- > An activity to be moved to the next day/month

When you reach the end of the month, take a look back and see all that you have achieved and what you would like to change for the next month. Amend the sections and habit trackers as appropriate, then set up a new monthly calendar, monthly goals and to-do list section, striking off or moving forwards any relevant goal.

健康

kenkō : health

●●○○○○○○

HEALTH | KENKŌ

Fall seven times, stand up eight – Japanese proverb

The Japanese have a phrase *shinshin ichinyo*, which translates as 'body and mind as one'. Rather than seeing the body and mind as two separate entities, as we often do in the West, *shinshin ichinyo* is about a deep interconnection between your body, mind and spirituality.[16] The way that you feel about yourself in your mind and your body has such an impact on everything else in the rest of your life that it seems like the perfect place to start to demonstrate how Kaizen can work in practice and transform your life. Rather than promoting another fad diet or extreme exercise trend, this section is going to be about practising self-love, attempting to banish some of the negative self-talk, and looking after your body and mind so that you feel more resilient when going out to tackle the stresses and strains of the outside world.

It feels like we are constantly being bombarded with different messages by the media about what we should be eating, drinking and how we should be thinking about and moving our bodies. One minute, eating lots of eggs is great for us – and then the next, eggs are terrible for us. One article will be detailing the benefits of running – the next will be telling us that it makes our boobs saggy. There is so much noise and misinformation, often written

by people with vested interests, that it is hard to decipher what is useful knowledge and what is made-up nonsense. On top of this, the growing number of 'health influencers' on social media with seemingly perfect lives, tanned bodies and incredible abs can make the world of healthy food and exercise seem very divorced from most people's reality. This is before we even get to the extortionate cost of 'boutique' gyms, and a day's worth of 'healthy' meals that get delivered to your door for the price of some people's weekly shop.

This can make the health world seem even harder to access for a person on a regular salary. Most people know, deep down, that they should be trying to achieve the elusive targets of eating better and doing more exercise, but it is hard to feel motivated to do so when the ideal seems so far-fetched, and expensive to boot. A common misconception of change is that it can be costly, but using the Kaizen method to slowly discover which exercises suit you and what you can afford each month means that you take on the changes at a pace that works for you.

And if you are, like me, a person who hated sports lessons at school, with traumatizing memories of having to go and stand on a freezing field holding on to a hockey stick for dear life while your teacher barked at you about how useless you are (just me?!), then the thought of an exercise class can be the most daunting thing. Thankfully, I hear from my schoolteacher friends that things have improved slightly on the PE-teaching front, but my fear of exercise still remains, especially knowing that classes will contain super-fit and toned people wearing sheer, bum-sculpting leggings and barely looking sweaty after an hour-long spin class.

This is why using Kaizen is a great way to motivate yourself to be healthier, as the way you approach getting fitter or eating better is incremental and hopefully not too scarily off-putting or expensive. Breaking down the initial steps and building up your exercise routine slowly means that it won't feel too daunting and it can be done almost anywhere. It is easier to motivate yourself to get started with better habits, to then step up to the next level, and eventually form a long-lasting good habit that you stick to.

Let's now explore the topic of health in more detail and show how Kaizen can work in practice.

EXERCISE

WHY SHOULD WE EXERCISE?

It is not news that we don't move around enough. The World Health Organization tells us that globally, around 31 per cent of people aged fifteen and over are 'insufficiently active' and that approximately 3.2 million deaths each year are attributable to insufficient physical activity.[17] These are sobering statistics, but it can be easy to acknowledge that you *should* be doing something to move around more, and feeling guilty when you don't, while still not actually doing anything about it. The thought of digging out your unused exercise gear and heading to a gym can seem like the worst thing in the world when it is cold and dark outside and there's a new Netflix series that has to be watched immediately to avoid spoilers.

HOW CAN KAIZEN HELP?

If your goal is to start exercising or to take up a new form of sport, then Kaizen is a great way to set and track your goals. There is no point in trying to run a marathon with no training or to start lifting a huge Olympic bar-bell in the gym having never done so before, as your body won't be prepared, and you physically won't be able to do it. Starting off small and building up from there will ensure that you don't overstretch yourself in the first instance. You will be less likely to suffer an injury and it will mean that you are less likely to be disheartened if you don't immediately reach your goal.

It might be that you are already sporty and have a clear idea of what exercise challenge you want to start. For everybody else – particularly those who are scarred from sports lessons at school with itchy gym kits and bullying teachers – the best thing to do is to try out a few activities and find something that works for you. The good thing is that exercise no longer has to involve getting hit in the face by a netball in the freezing rain while your classmates laugh at you.

First, think about what your main interests are. Do you enjoy dancing in your bedroom or walking in the park? You can easily step up these activities and turn them into proper exercise. Also think about your motivations and why you want to take up exercise. And from there, you can make some long-term, medium-term and short-term goals that work for you and your body. If you have bad knees, then think about what low-impact sports you could try, or if you have been feeling particularly anxious recently, then research yoga classes that are geared towards relaxing breathing techniques. Once you have an idea of things you might like to try, then it is time to put a plan in place to reach each step. Let's start off with some ideas for short-term goals and then use those as a springboard to think about the medium- and long-term goals.

SHORT-TERM GOALS

Find an unusual way to exercise. If you are a person who hates the idea of a treadmill, then why not investigate a swing dance class or a boxing class? Many gyms are waking up to the fact that people don't all want to exercise in the same way and there are often less traditional offerings, such as disco yoga, wrestling, circus skills, trampolining, hula-hooping and even daytime raving (alcohol-free, of course!). Thankfully gyms and local swimming pools are also realizing that people don't always want to sign up to a monthly membership and are now offering drop-in classes or pay-as-you-go memberships.

> *First Kaizen step: research the class and plan the outfit you will need to wear for it.*

Try out running, even if you've previously hated it. If the gym is your complete idea of hell, then there are plenty more outdoor or indoor options – and this is also where technology can come into its own. I have always hated running, but since returning from Japan, I have started to do small bits and pieces each week and am slowly building up the distance that I am able to run. I would be lying if I said I enjoy it all the time, but I definitely feel stronger and fitter for it, and it is a great way to catch up on podcasts and audiobooks too. Moreover, it is a completely free activity and can be done pretty much anywhere, although it is particularly pleasant if you have a nearby park or seafront where you can run. Kaizen is the perfect method with which to approach running, as if you try to do too much at the beginning then you will completely wear yourself out and potentially injure yourself. Trying to do a little bit at a time and slowly building up your distance is the recommended approach. There are lots of apps which can help you to plan routes and measure out distance.

> **First Kaizen step:** *plan the route that you would like to run in advance. All experts advise that you should start off mostly walking and then gradually introduce small runs intermittently into your routine. Be Kaizen in your approach and you won't go too far wrong.*

See what exercises are offered in your local park. One of the strangest and most compelling sights when I was living in Japan was seeing groups of people – often in huge numbers – exercising together in public spaces during the summer, usually early in the morning or when it got cooler later at night. In the 1920s, in honour of the coronation of Emperor Hirohito, Japanese radio started broadcasting *rajio taiso*, a sequence of simple exercises that people would congregate in public places to complete. The tradition continues to this day and involves a series of continuous stretches and light exercises in time to broadcasted music. Although this tradition has never taken off in the West, the idea of communal exercise very much has and there are plenty of local running groups, parks that offer exercise classes or boot camps, and community projects offering to help you get fit. If you live by the sea, then there are sea-swimming classes or various beach exercise classes too. Not only are these classes cheaper (or sometimes free) but you will have a ready-made group of other people to help spur you on and keep you motivated.

> *First Kaizen step: google your local park or recreation centre and find out what activities they are running.*

Use your commute to exercise. One of the best ways to get fit is to include exercise in your commute to work. This doesn't necessarily mean that you should sell your car and start walking ten miles every morning, but could you walk to the station rather than get a lift? Could you get off the Tube/train/bus one or two stops early and walk the rest of the way? Could you investigate cycling or running some of the way? Even something small like choosing to stand up on the train rather than sitting down, or taking the stairs at work rather than the lift is a way to make a difference. And then once you have got the hang of one small step, think about ways you can increase the level of activity you are doing.

> *First Kaizen step: get off one stop earlier and walk the rest of the way to work.*

Start gardening – yes, really! A number of studies have shown that gardening is great for your physical and mental health. The American Center for Disease Control classifies gardening as a 'moderate cardiovascular activity' and it can be a really effective way to keep fit. Rather than being sat on the sofa or at a desk, gardening forces you to constantly move about. The various movements it requires actually mimic those of regular exercise routines and it works out lots of different muscle groups. You might think that you are just pulling out a weed, but this actually doubles as a bicep crunch! If you are lucky enough to have your own garden or outdoor space then the thought of getting started and the constant upkeep can be daunting, especially if you are starting with a mess. Kaizen

is a great way to help tackle this. Rather than feeling like you have to make it perfect all in one go, why don't you devote just a small amount of time each day to one area and make that nice. If you don't have an outdoor space, check out whether parks or allotments accept volunteers to help out – most do – or there are plenty of schemes where you can assist elderly local people with their gardens. I'm sure many would be happy to accept help and you would be doing a good turn at the same time. You may find that you build better relationships with people in your community too: win-win!

First Kaizen step: decide on the first patch of the garden that you are going to work on or research a houseplant you want to buy.

Remember that walking, shopping and dancing all count! It sounds so obvious, but anything you can do to move around more is good for you. There are so many ways to get more movement into your every day, and hopefully you will find something to appeal even if you are the most exercise-phobic person, but if getting involved in organized classes or events is still too off-putting a thought, then how about just setting an intention to do anything which will get you off the sofa and outdoors? This can be to walk around the shops for two hours (have you ever noticed how much your feet hurt after a shopping trip?), to go dancing with friends and jump about lots on the dance floor, or even just to go for a walk with some music on for half an hour. You will find that getting out of the house and doing even just a small amount of activity is beneficial for both your body and mind.

> **First Kaizen step:** go for a walk for the duration of your favourite podcast.

LONGER-TERM GOALS

Once you have adopted a new exercise to try (and are hopefully enjoying it!), it is time to think about how you can step it up to the next level and set some medium- and long-term goals. Have a think about whether you can:

Increase the duration of the activity you are doing. If you are running for 2K each session, can you increase it to 3K? Can you set a target to work towards, such as running 5K without stopping (medium-term goal) or signing up for a half-marathon (long-term goal)? Or if you feel comfortable running 2K and don't want to run further, can you increasing the frequency of your sessions?

Increase the speed and/or intensity of the activity. Rather than increasing the time spent doing a certain activity, can you instead try to do more in the time that you have? Can you run the 2km in a faster time? If you have started to lift weights, can you start to build up the heaviness of the weights that you are lifting?

Flirt with high-intensity interval training (HIIT workouts). This is about mixing up the level of intensity during your workout, so that you have multiple short bursts of super-intense exercise (such as six rounds of thirty-second bike sprints or six rounds of one-minute road sprints), interspersed with short periods of low-intensity movement (such as one minute of walking or ninety seconds of easy spinning). If you want to try these out at home, there are hundreds of online workout tutorials to get you started. All you need is a stopwatch and a pair of trainers.

Do more activity, more often. Rather than relying entirely on one type of exercise, can you try something else as well and build it into your routine? Varying the types of exercise that you do will mean that you aren't putting too much pressure on one part of your body and will make injury less likely. Try stepping up the one session of activity each week to two or three (medium-term goal).

While making your plan, it is important to be mindful of potential pitfalls and excuses you will find to avoid exercising. Just being aware of them will mean that you are less likely to give in to them. Here are some tips for keeping on track.

Think about how you can fit the exercise into your routine so that you are most likely to keep going with it. If you are a morning person, then plan to exercise as soon as you get up and make time in your schedule for it. If you have time in your lunch-break at work, can you find some colleagues to join you for a run? If you would rather exercise as a way to let off steam in the evening, then schedule it for then.

Have the right kit. If it is freezing outside, then make sure you have some gloves and a long-sleeved exercise top. Invest in some cordless earphones, so that you can listen to music while running. Buy some leggings that won't fall down as you are running up a hill in the lunch-break exercise class with your colleagues (this is one I know from my own bitter experience!). Investing in some trainers that fit your instep and a good sports bra will save you pain later down the line. If you're like me, putting on some kit that fits you and makes you feel good inspires you to exercise much more so than an old baggy t-shirt and some saggy leggings.

Listen to your body. If your back is aching, then think of an exercise that could help to gently stretch it out. If you feel like you are pushing yourself too far, then reduce the intensity of the activity that you are doing. And always remember to do a proper warm-up and cool-down to avoid sore muscles.

Remember that variety is the spice of life. Doing the same thing over and over again will invariably lead to you getting bored. Try changing the route that you run or the scenery that you can see while you exercise. Mix up the types of exercise that you do and the music that you listen to.

Bring the outdoors indoors, or vice versa. If you know that bad weather outside is going to put you off, then think about how you can replicate the activity indoors instead. Can you plan a workout routine around your staircase or use the cans in your kitchen cupboard as weights (a top tip from my friend, who is a personal trainer!). Similarly, if you have been practising something like yoga or Pilates indoors, can you find a class which takes place in a park or try it in your garden instead? Note how being out in nature can transform your experience.

Involve others. We have an exercise club at our work, and having the peer pressure of my colleagues encouraging me to exercise at lunchtime definitely gets me out more than I would otherwise. If you have a friend who also wants to work towards a similar goal, try completing it together. When one of you loses motivation, the other one will be there to boost spirits.

Keep track. I keep a record of each of my exercise sessions in my journal so that I can look back at the end of each month and see how many sessions I have completed. Being able to see my progress on paper, as well as feel it in my body, helps to keep me motivated when I hear the voice in my head start to come up with excuses not to exercise. I also use a running app so that I have a more detailed breakdown of my times and distances. Choose whatever works for you, whether that is a wall chart, getting a friend or loved one to keep track, or even just dropping a quick email to yourself after every session. My friend does this and then keeps a folder in his inbox so that he can see at a glance when he has recently exercised and how each session went. He then reviews his progress each month.

Practise self-compassion. If you suffer an injury or if your initial enthusiasm starts to dip, it can be hard to keep motivated and tempting to give up completely. If this happens, remember the Kaizen approach by dialling back the amount of activity that you are doing to the bare minimum and starting to build it up from there. It is much better to do a small amount of activity than nothing at all. If you have an injury, seek professional advice on how long you need to rest and how to introduce activity back into your routine again.

Don't focus too much on weight loss. It may be that you don't have any intention to lose weight at all, but if that is one of your goals, then exercise is a good place to start. But having weight loss as your sole focus and motivation is never going to end well, especially as it completely ignores the other huge benefits of exercising. Building muscle changes the way that weight is distributed in your body so the number on the scales might not necessarily reflect how much stronger and healthier your body is. Instead, reflect on the following:

Are you sleeping better?
Do you feel stronger?
Do you feel fitter? For example, are you now able to run for a bus or after your kids without getting out of breath, or walk up the stairs at work without wanting to die?!
Do you feel like you have more energy?
Has it improved your mental health? For sufferers of SAD syndrome in winter, especially, getting out and exercising in the daylight has been shown to significantly improve your mood.
Do you feel inspired to eat more healthily?

DIET

This isn't a section about any sort of fad diet or about encouraging you to lose vast amounts of weight. And any major dietary changes you are thinking of undertaking should always be discussed with a doctor beforehand. But quite a lot of people would admit that they could be fuelling their bodies better and eating less crap. Applying Kaizen techniques to your dietary routine can be beneficial to those who want to make changes to the way they eat and their relationship with food – whether that is wanting to build strength, eliminate a health risk (i.e. if you have been told to cut down on a certain food or food group for health reasons), be more ethically and environmentally conscious of what you consume, or simply wanting to nourish yourself better. Rather than restricting your consumption or removing the pleasure from food altogether, the aim is to make incremental changes to the way you eat and drink in order to create and/or sustain a positive attitude towards fuelling both your mind and body.

Here are some suggestions for ways in which Kaizen can help you transform your eating and drinking habits in the short term, and we will then look at some medium- and long-term goals towards the end of the chapter.

DRINKING MORE WATER

The amount of water that you should drink each day depends very much on how much exercise you are doing, what you eat, your gender and how hot it is outside, but most people living in a moderate climate will need between six and eight glasses of water per day.[18] As well as water, it is possible to include milk, tea, coffee and any other sugar-free drink in your consumption. When it is hot or if you are hungover or busy with studying or at the office, it can sometimes be difficult to remember to drink water but using Kaizen to introduce it as a good habit into your routine is easy and beneficial. Here are a few ideas for how you can make some small steps towards becoming better hydrated:

If you hate the taste of water or want to make it more interesting, then flavour it with natural ingredients. Try adding lemons or limes to your food shop and then using them to flavour your water for the next few days. If the citrus taste is too bitter for you, then try cucumber or mint.

Link your water consumption to another moment in your day. A good way to automate your water drinking is to tie it to another habit that you already have. Plan to drink a glass of water every time you get up from your desk at work during the day. Or when you wake up in the morning, go straight to the tap and drink a large glass of water before you even have a chance to think about it.

First Kaizen step: try drinking a glass of water for every toilet trip you take over the course of one day.

Get technology to help you keep track. There are a number of apps that you can download on your phone to remind you to drink water – or set a reminder on your phone or work computer to alert you once an hour. It might be too much of an ask to drink every time you receive the alert, but even just being mindful of what you are drinking will make a difference to your mindset in the long run.

> **First Kaizen step:** *download a water tracking app and try to stick to its alerts for one day.*

Buy a fancy water bottle. Invest in a water bottle or thermos which you can use to store hot or cold drinks. You can then use this on your commute instead of paying for an expensive coffee or fill it with flavoured water and set yourself a challenge of finishing it by the time you get to work.

Remember that teas count too! There are hundreds of flavours of herbal tea and they all count towards your water consumption. Lots of teas contain useful antioxidants and benefit digestion as well. Invest in some new flavours to see if any become a favourite. I got really into drinking ginger tea in Japan and I am now *obsessed*.

Offset your booze. If you are drinking alcohol, try having one glass of water for every alcoholic drink you have and see if it makes any difference to how you feel the next day.

Get your water from your food. Try researching foods with heavy water content and add one item to your food shop. Lots of foods are rich in water, including cucumber, watermelon, grapes, strawberries, celery, lettuce, tomatoes, grapefruit. . .

Remember: Tune in to your thirst. If you feel thirsty then you definitely need to rehydrate. But over-hydrating can be dangerous too, so don't overdo it.

EATING LESS MEAT OR
BECOMING VEGETARIAN/VEGAN

Some of you might already be vegetarian or vegan, but many meat-eaters in this day and age also acknowledge that there are definite health benefits to cutting down on the amount of meat they eat, that it is more ethical and also better for the environment. As a result, many people are trying to reduce their meat consumption, and movements such as Veganuary and Meat-Free Mondays are becoming increasingly popular. There are also lots of vegetarians who are keen to make the leap to veganism but haven't quite been able to fully convert. Whatever change it is that you are trying to make, Kaizen can be an excellent tool to help with the transition, as it eases you into the change gradually and will mean that the change isn't too much of a shock to the system. Here are some ideas for first steps you could make:

⊙ *Decide on one night of the week when you will make a vegetarian or vegan meal.*

⊙ *Research one recipe that you would like to make and start to include it in your repertoire.*

⊙ *Choose one day where you are vegetarian at home and only eat meat when you are out of the house (or vice versa).*

⊙ *Investigate the meat and/or dairy substitutes on offer and switch one with a product that you already buy for a week.*

Once you have made one step towards your goal and decided that it is benefitting you (if it is!) then think about what next steps for progressing further towards your goal. Could you start being vegetarian for two nights per week rather than one? Or could you include one more vegetarian/vegan recipe into your regular meal routine? Or decide to eat veggie-only meals at home and then reserve meat for when you are at restaurants? There are lots of online articles and communities with plenty of tips to share; why not try asking your friends and/or family for recipe ideas too?

EATING MORE FRUIT AND VEGETABLES

The Japanese diet emphasizes the importance of fruit and vegetables, which is proven to be good for our health. A recent University College London study showed that people eating at least seven portions a day reduced the specific risks of death by cancer and heart disease by 25 percent and 31 per cent respectively.[19]

Not only is it healthier for us, but it is usually a cheaper diet than one which includes lots of meat products and items rich in fat. As in the section above about cutting down on meat products, Kaizen methods can be a good way to start to introduce more fruit and veg into your diet. Some ideas for how to do so are as follows:

Add 'secret' vegetables to your dishes. If you have a favourite recipe, can you think of a way to add one more vegetable into it? For example, could you add courgettes to a lasagne, or two types of beans to your chilli? Can you grate some carrot into a tomato sauce for a casserole or add some peas to a cheesy pasta dish?

Add a new vegetarian dish to your recipe rotation. Research one dish you could add to your repertoire that is mostly vegetable-based. Try a cauliflower-based pizza, a vegetable soup or an aubergine lasagne? Lots of Asian dishes lend themselves to added vegetables, whether that is noodles, soups, omelettes or stews.

Don't forget fruit and veg that you can store at home. Remember that frozen, tinned and dried fruit and veg also count. Think of one new way that you could consume fruit or veg as a snack and start to introduce it into your routine.

First Kaizen step: find a tin of vegetables or fruit that you haven't used in the back of the cupboard and plan a fancy recipe around it. Set yourself a challenge to make the dish feel more luxurious than it should do considering that it came out of the back of your cupboard!

CUTTING DOWN ON SUGAR

It is a truth universally acknowledged that consuming too much sugar and fizzy drinks is bad for your health and your teeth. The emphasis here is on *too much;* everybody deserves a treat every now and then, and sugar occurs in lots of natural products such as fruit too, so this is not to tell you to cut out sugar altogether. But health professionals recommend that sugar only makes up to 5 per cent of your energy in your diet.[20] If you feel like you need to cut down, then gradually reducing the amount of sugar you consume each day using Kaizen techniques will make the change in diet less of a shock to the system. Here are some ideas for small steps to go about reducing the sugar in your diet:

Read the ingredients. There are surprising amounts of sugar in ready-made sauces and condiments. Can you make your own curry sauce? Can you make your salad dressings from scratch once a week?

Be mindful of cereals or 'health foods' that contain hidden sugars. Some cereals are surprisingly high in sugar content. If you can't live without your morning bowl of granola, can you choose one day a week where you opt for a lower-sugar option and go from there?

Use fruit to sweeten items instead of raw sugar. If you like to add sugar to your cereal, can you replace it with fruit?

Try to cut down on adding sugar to hot drinks. If you regularly add sugar to hot drinks, try reducing the amount in really small stages.

> *First Kaizen step: make a cup of tea or coffee with a quarter of a teaspoon less sugar than you would usually use. Do you notice a difference? Do this for a week and then the next week reduce it by a further quarter.*

Cut down on fizzy drinks, even if they are 'low sugar'. Fizzy drinks mostly contain a lot of ingredients that are bad for your body, even if they are labelled as low-calorie or diet options. This isn't to say that they shouldn't be enjoyed as a treat, but if you are drinking them every day, then try to cut down. Each time you have a craving for a fizzy drink, see if there is an alternative that you can find to replace it with, such as fizzy water flavoured with fruit, or a new herbal tea.

PORTION CONTROL

This won't necessarily apply to everybody, but for those of us who find themselves eating too much in one sitting and who want to reduce their portion sizes, there are a number of ways to go about it. The Japanese Buddhist monk Shoukei Matsumoto in his book *A Monk's Guide to a Clean House and Mind* explains the technique of *hara hachi bu*, the Confucian idea of only eating until you are 80 per cent full, practised famously on the Japanese island of Okinawa. This idea sounds daunting so perhaps, as a first step, think of the day of the week you usually overindulge the most and decide that on that day you will only eat until you are 80 per cent full. If this works for the first week then why not try to extend this into a second? And after that, why not use this technique for more than one day in the week?

Other ideas could include:

Measure your food! If, like me, you end up making enough rice for an entire village when you only mean to cook for two, then investing in some measuring devices can help you to work out the correct portion sizes.

Look at your plate/bowl size. However big my plate is, I usually fill it entirely. A good way to reduce portion size might be to use a smaller plate!

> *First Kaizen step: use a smaller plate or bowl for just one meal a week and see if it makes a difference to how much you eat.*

Don't leave your leftovers in the pan. If you have made enough food to keep leftovers, then try to divide out individual portions into bowls or containers/freezer bags as soon as you have cooked and plated up. That way, you will have single portions in the future and it will discourage you from eating the leftovers all in one go.

Look for hunger signals. Like Shoukei Matsumoto says, the most important thing to do is to listen to your body and recognize when you are full or indulging for the wrong reasons.

MINDFUL EATING

We are all busy and often have to rush a sandwich or salad at our desks while continuing to plough through emails at lunchtime. Or we get home and rush around trying to make the kids three different types of meal while we mindlessly pick at different bits ourselves. But while we are eating and concentrating on another task, we are not focusing on what our body wants or needs. Mindful eating stems from ancient Buddhist practices, and encourages eating with awareness and concentrating on what you are consuming without judgement or criticism.

Mindful eating can be one of those things that sounds simple in practice but is easy to forget once you have been busy cooking a meal, are hungry and have a delicious plate of food in front of you. And remembering to sustain this practice over a whole meal and beyond is an even bigger challenge. This is where employing the techniques of Kaizen can be a great help. Some ideas for using Kaizen to start the habit of mindfully eating are:

Eat one item mindfully. For one week, pick just one item on your plate each day and concentrate on every mouthful as you eat it. Once you have mastered this, extend this to two items per day, and so on.

Eat at the table without distractions. Choose one day a week to eat at a table, put your phone in another room or on airplane mode, and just sit and enjoy eating in silence. Think of the sensations that you are feeling as you eat – when are you half-full? What tastes do you particularly enjoy? etc.

Concentrate on the first three mouthfuls of your morning coffee. If your schedule won't allow you to eat your meals without distractions – if you have young children or busy work commitments, for example – then how about starting with drinking mindfully instead? Try drinking a cup of tea or coffee and concentrating on just the first three mouthfuls.

Really focus on your food prep. Chop, cut and grate mindfully! Instead of just acting on autopilot when preparing food, how about concentrating on the sensation of chopping or grating for one minute?

LONGER-TERM GOALS

These practices will encourage you to have a more mindful attitude towards the way that you eat; you should feel more connected with what you are preparing at mealtimes and how it nourishes you. Make sure that changes happen gradually and fit in with your existing routine if you want to make a lasting difference. If your body thinks that you are depriving it, then it becomes harder to keep it up.

Track your progress and reward yourself when you reach certain
milestones. And if you slip up and overindulge or fall back into
poor habits, don't worry – you can easily pick up your new habit
again, but perhaps this time try making the change even more
incremental than before. Making changes to your diet should never
feel restrictive; rather it should be about gaining pleasure from what
you are preparing and eating, safe in the knowledge that your body
and mind will feel better as a result.

Think about your relationship to food and the changes that you
want to make in the long term. It could just be that you want to
feel better in your mind and body. Or maybe you want to cut out
a certain item completely, such as meat or fizzy drinks. Track your
progress and see where it leads.

SLEEP

Getting a good night's sleep is essential for our mental and physical health. Rather than being a time when the body completely shuts down, as is sometimes said, it is actually an active time when your body repairs cells, processes information and strengthens itself. Many of the exact ways in which this happens are still a mystery to scientists, but they all resolutely emphasize its importance for good health and wellbeing. The National Sleep Foundation lists a number of reasons why we need sleep, including:

- *Helping us to solidify recent memories*
- *Storing and processing long-term memories*
- *Growing muscle*
- *Repairing tissue*
- *Producing hormones*
- *Restoring and rejuvenating.*[21]

It is easy to acknowledge all of these benefits but if, like me, you suffer from bouts of insomnia, actually going about having a good night's sleep is another matter. The amount of sleep you need each night is different for every person, and very dependent upon your age and how much activity you have undertaken during the day. Most people will need between seven and nine hours every night. Almost everybody will have intermittent bouts of insomnia but if you are finding that you still feel really tired even after several nights of proper sleep or are regularly sleeping for less than six hours per night then do, of course, contact your doctor or a sleep specialist.

For people who think they could benefit from even slightly improved sleep, then Kaizen techniques are a great way to alter your existing sleeping habits and adopt a new, healthier bedtime routine. Not getting enough sleep or waking up in the night for long periods can be caused by external sources of stress: worries about work, friends, family or big life changes, such as getting married or moving house. This book contains lots of tips on how to use Kaizen to reduce these sources of stress and better cope with them when they do arise – but there is also lots that can be done to improve your bedtime routine and environment itself in order to promote a good night's sleep.

Before making any changes to your routine, a good place to start is with a sleep diary. Keeping a diary for a week will give you a general overview of how you sleep and will identify any issues or particular triggers for bad sleep.

HOW TO MAKE A SLEEP DIARY

Each morning for one week, make a note of the hours you fall asleep and wake up, how many hours of sleep you have each night in total, and whether you were awake for any period. It is also a good idea to rate the quality of your sleep out of ten. Our phones now have functionality that can help to track sleep, although the benefits of removing technology from the bedroom may outweigh the insight gained. Once you have the information about your sleep patterns, have a think and note down any factors which could have influenced the quality of your sleep in a good or bad way. For example:

Did you have any stimulants (caffeine, alcohol, nicotine) within two hours of going to bed?
What was the temperature of your room?
How light/dark was it? How noisy was it?
How messy is your room?
Did you look at any screens before going to bed?
Is there anything you were/are stressed or worried about?

You can either make a diary on paper, create a spreadsheet or use a sleep-tracker app on your phone to fill in the details. Although this will initially take a little bit of time, having a week's worth of information about your sleep patterns in front of you will mean that it is much easier to see where you might be going wrong and what external factors you can adjust to promote better sleep. Also note whether there are any differences between days when you are working/studying and your days off.

Sleep specialists recommend trying to keep to a regular daily sleep routine that doesn't fluctuate too much between weekdays and weekends. They advise that you try to go to bed at the same time and wake up at the same time every day, whether that is Monday or Saturday. And this is where Kaizen can be really helpful. It might seem daunting to try to change your whole sleep routine in one go, but making one small step at a time will encourage you to adopt better bedtime habits – and hopefully once one change starts to make a difference, then you will be motivated to make more. Over the page are some ideas for small changes that you could make to your sleep routine, both in terms of the environment in which you sleep and the actions you take before bedtime to promote sleep.

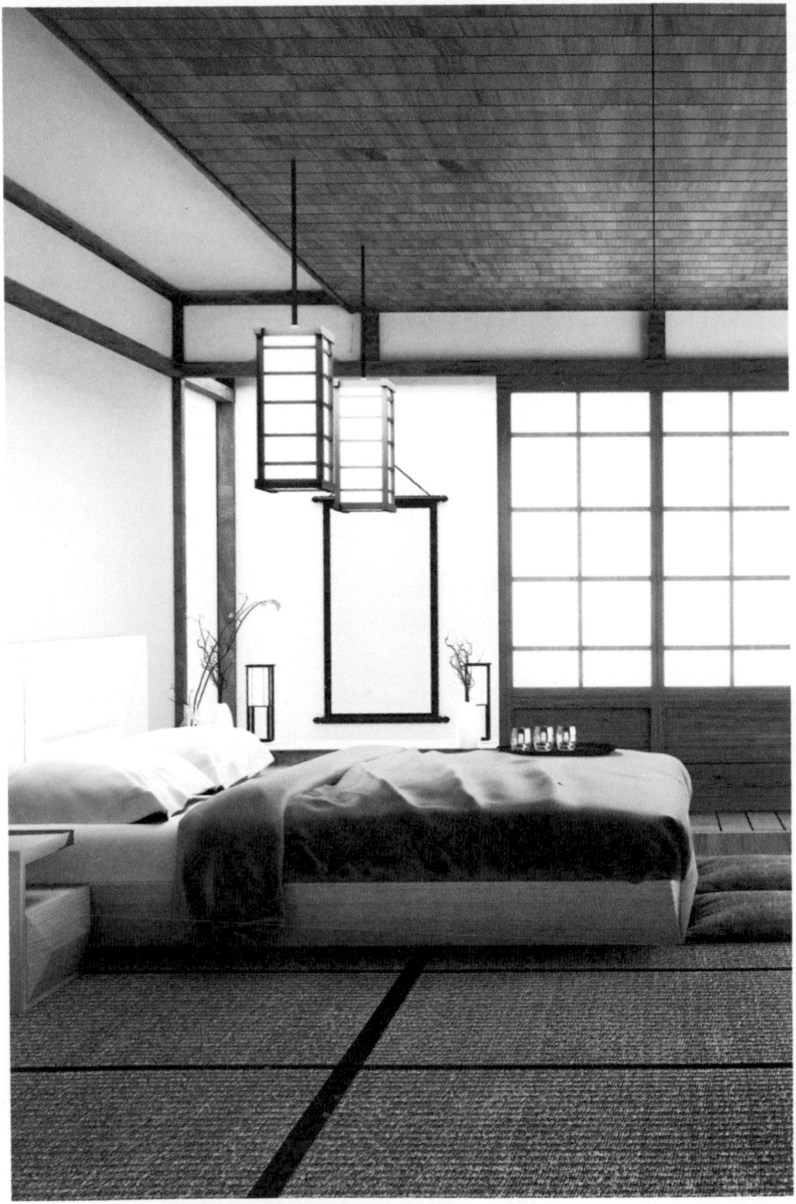

SLEEP ENVIRONMENT

Having your bedroom as a calm, clean environment free from clutter and external interruptions is key to good sleep. If you are really busy or tired then the thought of having to entirely transform your bedroom into a minimalist, serene paradise might seem too big an ask, but there are some small things you can do to make a difference. And once you have adopted one change, then try another to see if it makes even more of a difference.

Declutter your room. Your room should be calming. Designating it as a decluttered space which you use exclusively for either sleeping or sex will help to promote good sleep.

> *First Kaizen step: you might not always have huge amounts of time to tidy your entire room before bed, so set a timer on your phone for five minutes and just tidy up the area around your bed, so at least that area is free of clutter.*

Change your sheets regularly. Changing your bedsheets once a week or at least every fortnight can help to promote good sleep.

> *First Kaizen step: if you are really tired and the idea of changing your entire bed linen feels too much, then just change your pillowcases and/or bedsheet. The rest can be done another day!*

Block out noise altogether. If your street or building is noisy then try sleeping with ear plugs and see if it makes a difference.

Play relaxing noises while going to sleep. If you have trouble getting to sleep then try playing a relaxing sleep playlist or white noise (lots of sleep apps have these, along with YouTube and Spotify).

Shut out the light. Your room should be as dark and cool as possible. If you can't afford blackout blinds or thick curtains and find the room too bright, then try sleeping with an eye mask and note any differences to the quality of your sleep.

Sort out your mattress. If you think that your mattress could be what is causing issues, start to save a small amount (say, the price of a sleep-depriving coffee) each day towards a new one. Or if you are renting, then try asking your landlord to provide a new one. If a new mattress is out of your price range, then consider investing in a mattress topper, which are much cheaper and can make a big difference.

Surround yourself in some nice smells. Scents like lavender and bergamot have a calming effect. Find a scented candle, pillow spray or aroma diffuser and see if making your room smell nice makes you have a better night of sleep.

BEDTIME RITUALS

As well as making sure you create the optimum sleep environment, there are certain changes you can make to your actions in the period between returning home and going to bed in order to promote better sleep. As babies and children, we are coaxed (and occasionally strong-armed!) into a set bedtime routine, but as adults we often forget to perform such rituals, in favour of scrolling through

Instagram or binge-watching the latest boxset. Here are some ideas for ways in which you can improve your pre-bedtime routine:

Get out the loungewear. When you get home, immediately change into comfortable clothes to relax you and encourage your body to start to shut down.

Have a soak. Try having a warm bath or shower before bedtime – perhaps with added lavender oil – and see if it makes a difference to your sleep quality.

Take off your make-up. If you don't have time or the inclination to have a full bath, then try taking your make-up off as soon as you get through the door and apply a soothing face mask.

Hide your phone. Having phones and laptops in your bedroom can be a huge distraction. Try sleeping with your phone in another room and see if it makes a difference — or if the thought of that is too terrifying(!), then at least put it on airplane mode for when you are asleep.

Have a communication blackout. In the same vein, try to avoid social media or work emails for at least two to three hours before going to bed to minimize interactions whirring around your head.

> *First Kaizen step: have a few nights of a complete social media and communication 'blackout' and register if it has an impact upon the quality of your sleep.*

Be organized. Organizing yourself for the next day can be hugely beneficial for sleep in that it declutters your brain and gives you less to worry about the coming day. Try packing your bag, sorting out your breakfast items and/or packed lunch, and hanging up your outfit for the next day and see if that makes any difference to your sleep.

Be a bedtime yogi. Try doing some gentle bedtime yoga or meditation exercises before bed to help to promote sleep. There are lots of tutorials online or you can use a meditation app. Remember to keep it to very light exercises so that you don't overstimulate your mind and body too much before bedtime.

> *First Kaizen step: for one week, try meditating for five minutes before bed.*

Do a 'brain dump'. If your brain is still whirring, another idea is to get a piece of paper and write out a 'brain dump' of everything that is on your mind from that day. It doesn't have to be anything coherent or fully formed – just write out everything that is troubling you. This can also be a really useful exercise if you wake up in the middle of the night and are unable to go back to sleep.

Read a good book. Just six minutes of reading before bed has been shown to reduce stress levels by two-thirds and promote good sleep.[22] Choose a couple of nights of the week where you read before bed rather than look at a screen and see if it makes a difference.

Be kind to yourself. You can do absolutely everything right and there may still be a way that your body decides to rebel against you and give you a bad night's sleep. So don't beat yourself up if you have any setbacks when trying to improve your sleep routine. Simply focus on one small thing you can do to improve your sleep the next night. Keeping track of your sleep and the impact of any changes to your routine is key to identifying the ways in which your body is responding to the slight tweaks in your behaviour before bed and in your sleep environment.

BREATHING EXERCISE FOR SLEEP

For the times when you can't sleep, I am going to share with you a short breathing exercise that I find helps me when it is 3am and my mind is racing with nonsense thoughts. What yogis refer to as Moon Breath or *Chandra Bhedana* involves breathing in through your left nostril only. The left side of your body is thought to be associated with the nervous system, and so Chandra Bhedana has been traditionally used to calm it down and promote sleep. Here is a short exercise that you can do anywhere:

1. Sit upright or lie down, whichever is more comfortable.
2. Close your eyes and relax your eye sockets. Imagine your eyeballs are swimming in cooling pools of water.
3. Close your right nostril with your right thumb.
4. Rest the second and third fingers of your right hand in your right palm and extend your fourth and fifth fingers.
5. Breathe in through your left nostril and then close it with your fourth finger of your right hand, while releasing your thumb from your right nostril and breathing out through your right nostril.
6. Regulate your breath and keep repeating this action for a couple of minutes until your breathing is really slow and you feel more relaxed.
7. Hopefully your brain will feel less wired and you will be able to fall asleep.

A variation on this is to alternate the nostrils as you perform the exercise. This is called *Nadi Shodhana* or alternate nostril breathing and is a really simple way to quickly quieten the mind and settle your emotions, so is a useful exercise to have up your sleeve during moments of anxiety or stress. It really helps to focus the mind and press the reset button on your nervous system.

YOUR MORNING ROUTINE

It is all well and good perfecting your bedtime routine and having a perfect night's sleep, but not if this is then ruined by a frantic morning rushing around before work and stressing yourself out before you even get there. Some people will be reading this and will be unable to recognize this last-minute dashing around in the morning, but most of us will probably acknowledge that we could benefit from a more relaxed routine first thing! Getting to work or college and feeling calm and free of frazzle will mean that you are

able to start the day in a more relaxed manner and you will feel more capable of taking on whatever the day might throw at you. Or if you are a freelancer or somebody who works regularly from home, instigating a strict morning routine before opening up your laptop can make a positive difference to your productivity. Here are a few ideas for ways in which you can use Kaizen techniques to form good morning habits.

Get rid of annoyances. Have a real think about sources of stress in your morning routine and decide upon something you can do to eliminate just one source of stress. For example, if you find yourself getting annoyed by a certain breakfast DJ on the radio or a politician on breakfast TV news, could you try listening to a calming playlist or a podcast instead? See if making this switch for a week makes a difference. I have recently taken to playing a morning music playlist rather than listening to politicians arguing on the radio and it has had a huge effect on my stress levels.

Get out of bed five minutes earlier. Try setting your alarm just five minutes earlier and see if it makes a change to how rushed you feel getting out of the door. If this works, try extending this further by five-minute increments each week. Just having a bit more time to get your belongings together can have a huge impact.

> *First Kaizen step: set your alarm five minutes earlier every day for a week.*

Exercise early. If you want to start doing more exercise, research early-morning classes in your local area or go for a short run first thing. After one session, analyse how it makes you feel – are you more energized for the rest of the day? If you can't commit to a full class, then try doing some small stretches or a short online HIIT workout.

> *First Kaizen step: get up thirty minutes earlier one day a week and use the time for exercise.*

Have a mindful morning. Try practising five minutes of mindful breathing first thing when you wake up and notice if you feel calmer during the day. If you don't have time to commit to a full mindfulness practice, then try doing a part of your regular morning routine in a more mindful manner – for example, really concentrate on shampooing your hair or cleaning your teeth. If your mind starts to wander, then bring it back to the activity.

'Brain dump' in the morning. Similar to the 'brain dump' recommended in the pre-bedtime section (see page 98), try emptying your brain by writing down all of the thoughts that immediately spring to your mind when you first wake up. This can be anything from the crazy dream you had about cats to reflecting on the quality of sleep you had.

> *First Kaizen step: keep a notebook by your bed and write down all of your thoughts first thing in the morning for one day per week.*

Start a morning journal. If you want to adopt a more formal journaling practice, then each morning for one week try writing down your answers to the following three questions: What are you looking forward to today? What are you worried about today? What are you grateful for today? At the end of each day, look back on the three things you wrote in the morning and see if your day has panned out as predicted. See if there are lessons to be taken from this, for example, do you often catastrophize potential problems that turn out to be fine in the end?

Make time for breakfast. My mum always nagged me to have breakfast when I lived at home and many years later I can finally see that she was right! Research suggests that people who eat breakfast are slimmer, as they tend to eat less during the day – particularly fewer high-calorie snacks.[23] If you skip breakfast because you feel like you don't have time, try introducing a quick breakfast item, such as a smoothie, into your routine and see if it makes a difference to your hunger and energy levels throughout the day. If you are finding mornings are always too rushed, try doing some breakfast prep the night before. Chop some fruit the night before that you can just blast into a smoothie in the morning. Or try preparing an overnight oats pot.

> *First Kaizen step: think of a breakfast recipe that you would really like to eat and get up slightly early one day to make it. Did having that extra little bit of time to yourself to eat something delicious make a difference?*

Hydrate when you first wake up. If you don't have time to make proper food, then you should at least find time to have a snack and to hydrate yourself properly. Try adding in an extra glass of water to your existing routine. Can you have one as soon as you get out of bed? Or just before you get in the shower? Or leave a bottle by the front door so that you remember to take it for your commute?

Keep your phone on airplane mode. For one week try getting showered, dressed and ready for work without looking at your phone or reading the news until you leave the house. Does having some time to yourself first thing without external distractions make you feel calmer?

HOW TO DO A DIGITAL DETOX

We are living in an age when we are constantly expected to be 'on'. We are more connected than ever, but with this increased connectivity comes more pressure to be available at all times. Having 'read receipts' on our messages and information about when we were last available on messaging apps and social media means it is harder to switch off and not feel the need to immediately reply to people. When we have to use our smartphones for work as well as for our social lives, this pressure can be even greater and negatively affect our work–life balance.

We have already looked at some of the ways we can reduce the amount of time we spend looking at screens first thing, during our lunch-breaks and before bed, but for those of us who have the constant need to have our phones within reaching distance, limiting the time spent looking at and thinking about our phones is definitely to be encouraged. A recent study showed that the average American checks their phone forty-seven times a day, and one in ten people check their phone during sex(!).[24] And unsurprisingly, smartphone addiction is now a recognized condition. Tech companies specifically design products to be addictive and hard to live without, and evidence shows that they are succeeding in their aim.

We might all know that one person who still uses a phone from ten years ago without the internet (and don't they always seem happier?!) but most of us will admit that we are too dependent on our phones. Have you ever got home from work and thought you didn't have the time or energy to watch a film or read a book, but then get to bedtime and realize you have been scrolling mindlessly through your phone for hours without even noticing? Or have you been out for dinner with a friend and watched as they stop the conversation to check their phone every time a notification goes off? Do you feel anxious if you are in another room in the house to your phone and might miss a notification? Even if you don't feel that using your device has a detrimental effect on your mental health, do you think that your phone usage is sapping time and energy away from people and goals that matter?

Some people go to extreme measures to try to cut their attachment to their phones. There are now countless silent retreats or digital detox camps, where you pay a huge amount of money to 'go analogue' for a certain period of time. While these are undoubtedly effective ways in which to break up with your phone, there are also lots of smaller, less extreme (and less expensive!) actions you can take in order to make yourself slightly less reliant on your screens.

This isn't about rejecting social media and messaging altogether, but about finding ways in which you can engage with your phone without it taking over your whole life. It's about interrogating how you use your phone and how it can provide you with a meaningful connection with the outside world. And this is where Kaizen techniques can be very effective. Rather than dramatically going from constantly using your phone all the time to quitting it altogether, here are some ideas for starting to control your phone usage rather than letting your phone control you:

Track your usage. There are now various ways in which you can track your phone usage, including a number of apps specifically designed to do so, and so it might be worth doing this in the first instance in order to see how much you use your phone during the day. See which apps you use the most, and at what time you use your phone most heavily – you might be surprised by the results.

Install a detox app. There is a certain irony in using phone apps to reduce your amount of digital procrastination but try installing Forest (or others) and cutting the WiFi connection on your computer or phone for a certain amount of time, or switching to airplane mode. Do you get more work done? Do you find it easier to concentrate on tasks when you're not flitting between different websites and messenger services?

> *First Kaizen step:* install a detox app for one day and see what a difference it makes to your phone usage.

Leave your phone alone for an hour. If you find it hard to be apart from your phone, try leaving it in a different room or in your bag for an hour without looking at it. Or put it on airplane or do-not-disturb mode. Once the time is up, analyse how you feel. Did you miss anything important that couldn't wait until later? (The answer is probably 'no'.) What did you get done in that time period instead?

Delete or reorganize your apps. Try deleting social media apps from your phone and instead access them from your laptop or desktop computer. Do you use them as frequently? How has it changed the way that you think about them? If you don't want to delete them long term, then could you save them all in one folder which isn't on the front screen and as easy to access? Or change your phone's colour settings to grayscale so that the apps look less sheeny-shiny? Making your brain stop to think before using them will almost undoubtedly affect how automatically you reach for them when you unlock your phone.

> ***First Kaizen step:*** *reorganize your social media apps so they aren't on your phone home screen.*

Turn off notifications. Rather than having email and/or message notifications pop up on your phone, choose certain times of day when you are going to check them. This should reduce your immediate urge to reply instantly to everybody.

> ***First Kaizen step:*** *turn off your notifications for one day and reflect on how you feel afterwards. Has it made you feel less anxious? Did you use your time better?*

Switch off at mealtimes. If you spend mealtimes scrolling through your phone it can mean that you aren't always concentrating on what you eat or who you are eating with. Try having one mealtime where you ban devices and see what a difference it makes. Did you think more about your meal and enjoy it more?

Give a compliment IRL. Do you find that you are 'liking' things your friends post on social media but rarely compliment them in real life? Engaging with people in real life can be more rewarding than just mindlessly clicking the 'heart' button on Instagram.

> **First Kaizen step:** *send a message to one of your friends telling them something you like about them.*

Have a group phone amnesty. If you are out with friends or at home with family, how about having a 'phone amnesty' and keeping everybody's devices out of view for a certain amount of time? Does it have an effect on the quality of your conversation and attention that you pay each other?

These tips are all very small things you can try in order to see if they make a difference. The idea isn't to be a complete social hermit, but to be more mindful of your phone usage and how it can harm your concentration levels and the relationships with those around you. Making small adjustments to your phone habits can have a transformative effect. It can help to reduce your anxiety, sleep better and connect with people on a less superficial level.

SOCIAL MEDIA AND SELF-ESTEEM

All of the previous sections have talked about ways in which you can improve your physical health, and the link between this and your mental health is, of course, inextricable. Eating healthy food, moving your body about more, sleeping well, getting lots of daylight and keeping away from screens will inevitably have a positive effect on your mental health too. Coming back to the Japanese phrase of *shinshin ichinyo*, your body and mind should be treated as one entity.

But in our current image-conscious society, where we can open an app on our phone and instantly see our peers' carefully curated lives and celebrities living it up on superyachts in Mykonos, it can be very easy to feel inadequate and rubbish about ourselves, however much we are doing all of the right things. There will always be somebody with more glowing skin, having more fun at their birthday party or achieving more success in their career than you. Although social media has democratized who we can look at, it still often means we are inundated with images of thin, white, privileged, able-bodied people, who aren't representative of society as a whole.

This is nothing new, of course, with women's and fashion magazines' long history of using underweight, Photoshopped models and their frequent pedalling of an unobtainable lifestyle, but now social media has entered the fray. As well as comparing yourself to models and celebrities, it is now easy to pit yourself against your friends and colleagues. With one click of a button on our phones we can see heavily filtered Instagram posts and

Facebook statuses about how great a night out your ex-boyfriend had on Saturday. If you're lying in bed in an old t-shirt with your hair stuck to your face this can make you feel far worse. (I speak from experience!)

The study of the impact of social media on mental health and self-esteem is still very much in its infancy, but charities are becoming increasingly concerned about its effects, particularly on women. A study by Gothenburg University of Swedish Facebook users uncovered that the more time women spend on the site, the less confident and happy they feel.[25] Another study by Penn State University concluded that looking at selfies had a negative effect on self-esteem. From my own experience, and from talking to my friends and colleagues about it too, social media is undoubtedly something which affects our self-esteem[26] and we all recognize that we start to feel better about ourselves if we take regular breaks from it.

HOW TO STOP FEELING QUITE SO SHIT ABOUT YOURSELF

Everybody's self-esteem will be affected by different things, and not necessarily just by social media. We are consistently inundated with messages about how we should look, speak and act from birth, and this is a constantly changing ideal. When this is coupled with social media, who can blame us if we struggle to keep up with the advice and feel good about ourselves?

On bad days, the world can seem to contain endless ways to make you feel rubbish about yourself. You can be feeling on top of the world, then suddenly be sent into a body-hating spiral by a horribly lit changing room in a clothes shop. It could be that somebody undermines you at work and your confidence plummets, or that you are a new parent and someone questions something you do with your baby.

And you may find that you respond differently to all of these things depending on your mood and mental health at that certain moment. A bad picture you see of yourself may get to you one day, but then on another day you could notice that you are smiling sincerely or your hair looks nice. Having good self-esteem is definitely not something to be taken for granted and is something that can see-saw from day to day. This is why it is imperative to do as many small things as you can to bolster your self-esteem and to try your best to ensure that your dips in confidence happen less and less often.

Many of the actions I have recommended already will help towards your goal of having good self-esteem. Eating well, exercising and mindfulness, and doing as much of a digital detox as you can manage, will all contribute to you feeling healthier, stronger and in a better place mentally. But sometimes you will still have a bad day no matter how many burpies you have conquered or carrots you have eaten. Our inner critic can put a negative filter on everything we do. We are never objective about ourselves. And this is where practising small steps towards both body positivity and self-love can be very beneficial. This next section includes lots of small ideas for when you are feeling down on yourself but which you can also practise in-between times, so that you become more resilient and better able to cope when you are next struggling.

Important note: Although having bad self-esteem isn't actually classified as a mental illness, many of its symptoms are the same. If you find that you are feeling completely hopeless, blaming yourself unfairly for an action, feeling hatred towards yourself or finding yourself completely incapable of doing things, then these can be symptoms of depression or anxiety, so do please go and consult a medical health professional.

TAKE STOCK

Take a step back and think about what the triggers are for you feeling bad about yourself.

If you can, try carrying around a journal with you for a week and make a note of each bad thought that you have about yourself and who or what has caused it. This won't be a pleasant task, but it might be very revealing.

Once you have an idea of the trigger(s) that cause you to feel bad about yourself, the first step is to see if there are any easy ways you can start to eliminate them.

⊙ If you have an overly critical friend/family member/colleague, would it help to have a word with them or write a note/email telling them how they make you feel? Half of the time people are unaware of their actions and might not even know that they are causing you harm. If you feel unable to open up to them, can you find a way to limit your contact with them? Life is short, and you should do all you can to fill your time with people who bolster you!

⊙ This same advice applies to romantic relationships. It could be that your partner has no idea that they are making you feel a certain way. If they respond negatively or you feel unable to talk to your partner in the first place, then this is a sign that you might not be in a healthy, balanced partnership.

⊙ If social media makes you feel deflated, try having a digital detox for half a day (see page 104).

⊙ There is lots of advice on how to combat stress at work in the next chapter. If you are struggling, try having a coffee with a supportive colleague, or create a 'compliments folder' on your computer desktop for saving any nice notes you receive about your work.

⊙ If you are feeling low because of a recent personal change, such as a relationship breakdown, this can make you feel very exposed, alone and raw. Look after yourself as much as possible and surround yourself with supportive people who can counteract any of the negative things you are thinking about yourself.

HOW TO DO A BODY SCAN

A body-scan meditation helps you focus on where you might be holding physical tension and can also reveal any built-up emotional tension. I often tense my neck and shoulders, and even just occasionally becoming conscious of that, taking a breath and lowering my shoulders makes a noticeable difference.

Try doing the activity below once a week and see if it has an impact. This is a good exercise if you are having trouble sleeping or if you want to relax before getting up in the morning. Let it take as long as feels comfortable – for some people this is five minutes, others might take half an hour.

1. Find a place that is relatively quiet and free of interruptions.
2. Sit or lie down in a comfortable position.
3. Close your eyes and become aware of your breathing. Start to steady your breath.
4. Starting at the top of your head and scanning down slowly, bring awareness to each part of your body.
5. First try to release any tension from your forehead, your temples and your ears.
6. Imagine that your eyes are bathing in pools of water.
7. Move on to your cheeks, jaw and neck, releasing each part as you go. (Keep breathing!)
8. Next up are your shoulders, your arms, your chest and your spine. When you reach your belly, be sure to breathe into it and release all of the tension from the top part of your body.

9. Next, scan down your pelvis, your bum and each leg in turn, until you reach your feet.

10. Bring awareness back to the breath and breathe into all of the areas of tension.

11. Finally, tense all of your body at once. And then release. How do you feel? Each time you perform the exercise, focus on the response that you get from each area of your body. Does it ache, hurt or feel stiff, or is it warm, cold or itchy? Or do you feel nothing at all (that's fine too!)? This exercise can sometimes cause negative emotions to rise to the surface and make you feel a bit tearful so don't worry if it does.

If you find that this exercise has helped to relax and de-stress you, try stepping it up by either increasing the frequency with which you perform it or the length of time that you spend doing it.

仕事

shigoto : work

WORK | SHIGOTO

We spend a lot of our lives at work, especially if we live in places with a culture of overtime and where people are reluctant to take their annual-leave allocation, such as the US and Japan. The Japanese even have a word, *karoshi*, which means 'death from overwork'. We are working longer hours than ever before, and technological developments now mean that we can be on the end of an email 24/7. To try to tackle this, France brought in a new law in 2017 giving employees the legal right to not check emails out of hours. But many other countries are lagging behind and burnout from overwork is a very serious problem around the world.

Achieving happiness and fulfilment at work is possible but not a guarantee. You can never fully control the people you have to interact with or what work problems might arise. What you can do, however, is create as pleasant an environment as possible and look after yourself both physically and emotionally to ensure that you are best placed to weather the inevitable storms that occur throughout the day. This is where Kaizen techniques can be transformative. Taking a step back to see what working habits don't serve you and trying out some new things to shake up your tired old routine can make a huge difference to your happiness levels during the day and to your work–life balance. Taking stock of how you feel about your career and the way it is progressing can be very illuminating

too, and can perhaps highlight areas in which you are unhappy or prompt you to think about a career change.

In this chapter I will look at some easy steps you can take to improve your current working environment, provide some tips on how to enhance your wellbeing at work, and also encourage you to think about the longer term and whether the career path you are on is the right one.

CREATE A PLEASANT WORKSPACE

For people who have to go into an office every day, it's hard to have total control over the environment that you are working in. You can leave your calming home, do all you can to make your commute as stress-free as possible, and yet still end up in a windowless cave with a sad-looking filing cabinet for company. Many workplaces are waking up to the fact that their employees are happier and potentially more productive if they enjoy the space that they are surrounded by, but many aren't or don't want to invest any budget in making positive changes. Whatever your situation, there are a number of really small things you can do to make your workspace a nicer and more stimulating environment.

As with everything Kaizen, the first thing to do is to take a step back and take stock. Think about ways in which you can make your working environment more pleasant. Have a look at your desk space and think about:

The lighting. Are you getting enough daylight? Do you have nice lamps or is it just horrible strip lighting overhead?

Personalization. Does the space feel like your own?

Green things. Can you see plants and trees?

Posture. Does your chair support you properly? Can you reach your keyboard without having to lean forward? Is the top of your screen at eye-level height?

Clutter. Do you have papers scattered everywhere? Is there an old gym kit or lunchbox festering underneath your desk?

Storage. Do you have enough and is it the right type?

Once you have done an honest assessment, think of very small ways that you could improve the space. In an ideal world, your office would pay for all of these improvements and it is always worth asking if there is any budget. You should also definitely consult your HR department or office manager if you are experiencing aches and pains from the way that you sit, or if you don't get any daylight. Over the page are some ideas for very small things you can try that will transform your day even if there isn't a huge budget.

Get as much daylight or white light as possible. Several studies have shown that employees without any access to natural light will get less sleep at night, report poorer sleep quality, feel less inclined to do physical exercise, and generally report a worse quality of life than their counterparts who do have access to natural light.[27] If you don't have access to natural light, then talk to your office manager or line manager about whether any changes can be made. Can you operate a desk rotation system with those who do have light desks? Or can the office invest in white lamps for those who don't?

Surround yourself with photos and uplifting things. Printing off a few pictures of friends, family or favourite artworks will infinitely liven up your workspace. Collect postcards when you go to art exhibitions and museums and print off pictures of holidays and fun times.

First Kaizen step: print off a picture or find a postcard that makes you feel happy and place it next to your desk.

Invest in some plants. A 2014 study by the University of Exeter of three workplaces in the UK and the Netherlands concluded that employees were 15 per cent more productive when they could see plants in their workspace.[28] Their memory retention improved and they reported feeling generally happier at work. Succulents are cheap, happy to be indoors and are very hard to kill (even for me!), so unlock your inner millennial and see if having a plant on your desk makes a difference to how you feel at work.

Go fully Japanese and get a bonsai tree! There are many shops that now sell bonsai trees – check out your local flower or plant shop.

Or if you are feeling craftier, make your own from a starter kit
– there are lots online.

Surround yourself with nice smells. Japanese businesses have long
espoused the benefits of having pleasant-smelling offices. A 1985
study by Professor Shizuo Torri at Toho University discovered that the
use of essential oils in the office can have a stimulating and relaxing
effect. The Shimizu Corporation, one of Japan's largest construction
companies, took on this study and started creating 'intelligent' offices,
which disseminate different smells into areas of the office to improve
efficiency and relieve stress. A reed diffuser or an aroma diffuser could
be a good alternative. Fill it with your favourite essential oil and note
how different you feel. If you sit near to others make sure that you
discuss their scent preferences beforehand!

Sort out the clutter. It might seem too large a task to try to sort out
absolutely everything in your office or desk space at once. So break it
down into very small steps. Once a week, allocate a drawer that you

wish to tidy for five minutes. If there is an old file that you haven't been through in years, take five minutes out of your afternoon to look through it and chuck everything you don't need away. The thought of having to do everything at once can feel like a huge mountain to climb so concentrate on one very small thing you can do.

> **First Kaizen step:** *clear out one of your office drawers and reflect on how much more zen you feel.*

Get your colleagues involved. This means you can all spur each other on.

> **First Kaizen step:** *try setting a timer for five minutes once a week and all tidying as fast as you can for that short period. Reward yourselves afterwards with a sweet treat.*

Make your storage look pretty. Endless cardboard boxes of files or old rusty wire trays can look hugely uninspiring, so think if there are any ways you can jazz up your storage. Lots of shops now sell very cheap wire baskets in fun colours or can you cover your existing boxes in wallpaper samples or cool posters that you like? Get creative and see how much it can transform your space.

Most people spend at least eight hours a day sitting at work and so it's important to try to make it as joyful as possible. If your office doesn't have the budget to make any improvements, can you organize a bake sale or some other event to raise funds to change the space?

DE-STRESSING YOUR COMMUTE

If you do have to commute to and from work, the section on exercise has already introduced the idea of using your morning commute to move about more, but have a think about whether there are any other ways that you can make your commute less stressful. Over the course of a week, try writing down at the end of each journey what the small sources of stress were, and then for each stress, think of a way in which it could be eliminated. This might not be possible for absolutely everything – there is no way to always account for somebody shoving their smelly armpit in your face on the metro or somebody eating fried chicken next to you at 8am – but do think of small ways you could improve your travels. Here are some ideas for short-term steps:

Alter your journey to a quieter route. Although this may take slightly longer, does it have an impact on your stress levels? Does getting a train that takes ten minutes longer but where you get a seat prove a more pleasant experience than being crammed on the faster train? Try this once and see if you notice a benefit.

Make a case for changing your work hours. Could you alter your work hours slightly so that you get to work earlier and leave earlier, or arrive later and leave later? More and more work places are waking up to the idea of flexible working hours. It may be that it helps a lot with childcare or helps with the fact that you are more productive in the morning or not a morning person at all. You may find that altering your working hours even by half an hour makes a big difference to the stress of your morning or evening routine.

Block it out! If the various sounds of people around you are
an irritant, then does travelling with some noise-cancelling
headphones make a difference? Can you investigate new podcasts or
soothing playlists that will change your experience?

Put down your phone. Could you use the time more effectively? Does
reading a book make you feel any different when you arrive at work?
Or can you spend the time learning a new language?

> *First Kaizen step: spend one commute with your phone turned off in
> your bag and read a novel instead.*

MAKE THE MOST OF YOUR BREAKS

If you're busy at work and in the flow of doing something, it is easy to just continue to plough on through, eat a Sad Sandwich at your desk, and not take any time out for yourself. Statistics show that only one in three workers takes a proper lunch-break, and this is proven to be bad for both your physical and mental health. Getting outside increases your vitamin D and serotonin levels, while eating mindfully rather than distractedly will mean that you take more time with your food and will appreciate it more. Here are some easy ways in which you can transform your lunch-break:

Exercise! More workplaces are now offering group exercise sessions or yoga/Pilates classes. If they don't already, can you see if there are other colleagues interested in a lunchtime exercise club? Not only is it bonding but having others to motivate you to step away from your desk will ensure that you keep up the habit.

Have a walk outside. Going for a walk can sound like such rudimentary advice, but escaping your desk and getting outside can make such a difference. Is there a local park nearby or a canal or river that you can walk along? If you work in a town or city centre, are there roads or areas nearby which you are yet to explore?

First Kaizen step: for one lunchtime per week, try getting outside for an hour.

Be a culture vulture. Are there any galleries or museums near to your work which you are yet to visit? Going during the week will often mean that it is much quieter, and you can explore in peace while also getting your cultural fix.

Read. Try spending one lunchtime a week reading a book and see if it makes any difference to how you feel when you return to your desk. Did it transport you to another world free from annoying emails? See if there is a local library that you can join – not only so you can you borrow books for free, but they often have relaxing reading spaces where you can really switch off.

Be prepared. How often do you finish your lunch and feel satisfied? Do you spend too much money at overpriced sandwich chains? If the thought of having to prepare your lunch every night or morning before work is too daunting, try introducing it into your routine once or twice a week. There are many recipes online for satisfying lunch ideas, or bring in leftovers from the night before. Investing in a stylish bento-style lunchbox makes the contents seem more desirable than an old takeaway container.

Give your nan* a call! Is there a friend or a family member who you haven't called for a while? Spending your lunch-break connecting with a loved one will be infinitely more satisfying than just scrolling through the internet for an hour and will let them know that you care too. **Insert applicable friend or family member here.*

First Kaizen Step: *try a five-minute lunchtime meditation.*

Go and get a bit zen. The office might seem like the last place that you should meditate, but can you find a quiet meeting room or breakout space? Or is there a bench or patch of grass outside that you can use? Taking some time out to relax your body and just concentrate on your breath can have transformative effects on how you feel for the rest of the day.

FIVE-MINUTE LUNCH-BREAK MEDITATION

Whether you work from home or are stuck in a stuffy office all day, taking five minutes out to concentrate on your breath and think about how you are feeling that day can have huge benefits, whether everything is going swimmingly or if you're having a total shitshow of a day.

I started taking up meditation after a bad break-up and found it really helped me to process my emotions – not by blocking them out but by acknowledging when I felt bad and accepting those feelings. It resulted in me being kinder to myself and – I think – handling the break-up better than I would have done otherwise. During a stressful patch at work, I also found it very useful to take a little bit of time out at lunchtime to meditate when it all got a bit much. I would return to my desk feeling much calmer and far more inspired to work hard in the afternoon.

There are plenty of guided meditation apps that you can download to your phone, or videos that you can stream on YouTube; these are particularly useful if you want to get into doing longer meditation sessions. If you are new to meditation though, and not sure if you'll like it, here is a really quick five-minute exercise to try. It is super-easy and can be done literally anywhere you like.

1. Find a quiet space to sit down where you are free of distractions. This can be in a meeting room at work, in your work canteen, on a bench outside, under a tree in the park, on the toilet(!) – wherever feels comfortable.

2.	Set a five-minute timer on your phone or watch.

3.	Close your eyes (or if you don't want to close your eyes in a public place then try to relax them and gently focus on a specific spot).

4.	Start to pay attention to your breathing. Is it shallow or strained in any way? Can you make it deeper? Do this for ten breaths.

5.	Then expand your awareness out to your wider body. How do you feel today?

6.	Once you have thought about how you feel and you have acknowledged any emotions, take out your awareness even further to the environment around you. What can you hear? Or is it just silence? Are there any smells?

7.	Finally, return to the breath and concentrate on slowly breathing in and out until the timer goes off. Your mind will probably start to wander during this part, but if or when it does, acknowledge the thoughts, let them pass over you, and then return to your breath.

8.	When the time is up, gently open your eyes (or bring your focus back) and take in your surroundings again. How do you feel? Are you calmer?

You may find that your mind tends to wander more on certain days, especially if you are particularly stressed. Don't panic if this happens, it is all part of the process. If you find this exercise useful then try introducing it into your lunchtime routine once or twice a week. If you find this beneficial then you can step it up by meditating more frequently or by adding on a few minutes to the time that you spend meditating.

HOW TO HAVE A BETTER WORK DAY

We have already talked about transforming your morning routine, your commute and your working environment, but all this effort is redundant if you then get to work and immediately feel stressed or out of control. There will almost always be minor irritations – certain colleagues who cook fish in the microwave or man-spread in meetings – but there are also practices that you, yourself, can change in order to manage your time better and achieve an improved work–life balance.

In order to establish some of the things you might want to change, it is a very good idea to take a step back and really interrogate the ways in which you are working. Could you be happier at work? What are your current grievances? Are there any 'quick wins' for ways that you can improve things?

Have a think about the following:

- *Do you have a good work–life balance?*
- *Do you regularly work over your contractual hours? If so, is it because you are expected to? Is there a culture of presenteeism?*
- *What are your relationships like with your co-workers? Do you like your boss? If you manage people, do you think that you do a good job of it?*
- *Do you like the company ethos in general?*
- *Do you feel challenged and motivated in your work?*
- *Do you take regular breaks?*
- *How do you feel at the end of the working day? Tired, thirsty, hungry, frustrated, unfulfilled, like you have done your best?*

Keeping a work journal that's purely dedicated to how you feel at work over the course of a week can be really illuminating. At the end of each day make a note of how you have felt at work that day and any problems that have arisen. Is there a particular person who is causing you grief? Did you manage to take breaks? etc. Once you have interrogated how you are feeling at work, think of some small actions you can take to improve your working life.

EMAIL ETIQUETTE

For most of us, emails make up a major part of our working life. They are a constant source of stress, seemingly screaming for our attention. I have always worked in very email-intensive jobs and at times have found it impossible to keep on top of them. They can't be eliminated completely, but you may find that being mindful of their effect on you and changing your attitude towards them can make a big difference.

Behavioural psychologists acknowledge that email is incredibly habit-forming because it mimics what is referred to as a variable-interval reinforcement schedule. In layman's terms, this means that each email demands our attention because we keep chasing the next interesting one. Perhaps one in twenty emails we receive will be something of note, but we will keep checking regularly in order to seek out the gratification of that one important email, even when the rest is made up of spam or people complaining that the men's toilet is blocked. In the same way that gambling addicts keep playing the slots in Vegas waiting for their windfall, we keep waiting for the next interesting email. It might not sound as harmful, but the unconscious compulsion to check emails – especially when you're not at work – can form a bad habit that can have huge effects upon your social and home life. Even at work, it means that you are constantly flitting between tasks and not getting in 'the zone'. Here are some small ideas for transforming your email etiquette:

Don't check email on the way into work. A study released in 2018 revealed that half of all office workers were checking their emails on the way into work.[29] You aren't getting paid for this time so make sure that it is all your own.

> *First Kaizen step: choose one morning a week where you don't check on emails or think about work at all until you reach the office.*

Turn off email notifications! Do you find that you are often working on one task and then suddenly an email pops up and immediately demands your attention? This happened to me a lot but then I (accidentally) turned off my email notifications and suddenly found that I could concentrate far more easily on one thing at a time. It was like Einstein's apple-tree moment, but only slightly less revolutionary!

Designate times of day to check email. This will depend on the nature of your work, but if you have a job that requires a mixture of tasks then think about whether you can be off email for periods of time each day in order to get the other tasks done. Rather than constantly trying to multi-task between answering emails and other tasks, you will find that you are far more productive if you concentrate on doing one thing well for a prolonged period. Close down your email and focus on a creative task that needs your full attention for a set period of time. Then return to your emails when you are done. I find that I have hardly ever missed anything by being away from my emails for half an hour or forty-five minutes. If people need you urgently, then they will ring or come to find you.

Keep only urgent things in your inbox. If you receive lots of emails every day and find that you have a humongous inbox that keeps you awake at night, try starting to keep only emails that you need to action in your actual inbox. Everything else can be filed into folders and searched for later. It can be hard to start doing this if you already have a huge inbox to clear, so try moving all of your inbox into a folder and then moving out the urgent tasks. You can then clear the messages in the folder when you have more time.

If you receive an anger-inducing email, leave it for half an hour. Replying straight away when you are full of rage will do nothing to calm down the situation (or you!). Take some time away from your screen or go to seek advice from a helpful colleague rather than feel like you have to respond instantly.

> *First Kaizen step: try this tip with your next annoying email and see if it has any impact upon how you feel.*

Would a phone call be better? I often find that so many of my tedious email chains spent endlessly pondering over various situations could have been resolved much more quickly if one of us had just picked up the phone. This won't be the answer every time, but it can save a lot of back-and-forth. You may also find that somebody who has a standoffish email manner may actually be lovely in real life and much more amenable over the phone than via email.

Go to talk to colleagues! Similarly, I used to find that colleagues who sat across the desk from me would email me questions when it would have been far quicker to just ask me out loud.

> *First Kaizen step: next time you have a question, be brave and go and find the person instead of emailing them.*

For most of us, email will have been part of our job for most of our working life, and old habits are very hard to break so don't try to introduce all of these techniques at once. The most important thing is to be mindful of your attitude towards email, notice when you are slipping into bad behaviour, and trying your best to switch off when you can (and/or get friends and loved ones to remind you of this).

LOOKING AFTER YOURSELF

We have already looked at ways to develop a healthy and productive commute and lunch-break, but also think about ways that you can look after yourself during the working day.

Be mindful of what you eat and drink at work. I am somebody who used to always get to the end of the day and be thirsty because I had drunk seven cups of coffee and not a single glass of water. Don't be like me! Try replacing your caffeine with water and having healthy snacks to hand for when you get sugar cravings.

> *First Kaizen step: try to tie filling up your water bottle or glass to a regular activity you do, such as going to the toilet or speaking to your boss.*

Have breaks. Make sure that you leave your screen for at least five minutes every hour.

Go outside! Even if the sun isn't out and it is miserable outside, you can still get a hit of vitamin D and boost your serotonin levels. It will make you feel infinitely better.

Improve bad working relationships. We are all human and if you are working in an office with lots of different personalities – most of whom you probably didn't choose to work with in the first place – then it is inevitable that there may be certain people who you don't get on with. It can be easy to get completely bogged down by annoyances with certain people or feel impotent if you have a toxic relationship with a colleague. Take a step back and think about whether there is anything you can change about your current

environment to improve things. Can you discuss your issues with somebody from another department who might be more objective? Or could you reorganize the structure of a meeting so that it is harder for a certain person to dominate? Finding someone to confide in may help you solve the problem.

Surround yourself with positive influences. You might not be able to avoid colleagues who you don't like altogether but you can do something about proactively surrounding yourself with positive and supportive people. If there is a more senior colleague who you admire, then I'm sure they won't mind if you take them out for a coffee to pick their brains or ask for advice. Similarly, if there is somebody in a different department who you sense that you might get on with, then invite them for lunch. Having supportive people you can turn to when work is tough or you have a sticky situation with your boss can be so helpful.

ATTENTION: FREELANCERS!

If you are a freelancer or work from home, it can be easy to work
propped up in bed with your laptop burning into your lap until you
realize that the only human contact you have had all day was with the
postman and that you haven't worn anything but loungewear since
the weekend. (Can you tell that I talk from experience?)

If you are fortunate enough to have space for a home office, then use
some of the tips in the previous section to create your own calming
work environment. Often home offices become multi-functional
rooms that double as a dumping ground for clothes and/or arm
weights for when you *definitely* start that routine to get 'Michelle
Obama arms', so see if you can change the space so that it is
exclusively your own inspirational place to work.

For those people who don't have an office space, then do try to at least
move out of your bedroom to work. Separating out where you work
from where you relax is crucial for achieving good sleep and indicating
to your brain that you are now in 'work mode' when you set up in the
morning.

Know when you work best. Some people are able to sit at a table
from 9am until 8pm and work consistently for that amount of
time until they are done. I am not one of these people. One of the
benefits of being in control of your working time is that you can
tailor it to how you work best. Are you an early riser and more able
to concentrate in the morning? Then get up at 6am and work until

lunchtime. If you hate mornings then don't force yourself to get up early, but structure your day around a later finish and don't feel guilty about it.

Have a strict routine. While you should be flexible with your schedule according to how you work best, it is still imperative that you stick to as much of a routine as possible. If you find that you are more creative in the mornings, then allocate your creative time for then and save the boring admin tasks for the afternoon, or vice versa. And try to always finish at a certain time each day so that you clearly denote which hours are your work time and which are your leisure time. It can be so easy to let your work bleed into your personal life, so be sure to allocate set working hours, stick to them, and let others know of them so that they don't try to encroach into days or hours when you're not working.

Get out of bed. Not everybody will have the luxury of a home office but physically getting up and moving into another room will indicate to your brain that it is now time to work. It will also help your sleep environment by banishing any reminders of work from the bedroom.

Change your scenery. I found that whenever I was in a creative rut, just going and working in a new place – whether that was the foyer of a museum, on a bench in the park or a cool coffee shop – really helped. It doesn't have to be every day, but switching up your surroundings can have a huge effect on your creativity and productivity.

> *First Kaizen step: designate one day a week to working in a different place to where you usually work.*

Remove reasons for procrastination. There are now lots of free programmes you can download that will restrict social media and/or access to the internet altogether for a set amount of time. I am the sort of person who can accidentally fall down a social media 'hole' for hours without realizing it, so I find that proactively restricting my access to the internet really helps my concentration.

Schedule in procrastination time. If you like to scroll through the news or Instagram for an hour first thing, then accept that this is the case and schedule it into your plan for the day. It will remove the associations of guilt and mean that you then have time to concentrate afterwards.

Accept that you will have off days. If you have a day where you feel creatively blocked or too tired and overwhelmed by what you have to do, this doesn't matter so much in an office where you are getting paid a regular salary. But if you are working for yourself and having to organize your own time then it can make you feel SO guilty. Be gentle on yourself. If you are able to close your laptop and give it a rest, then do so and start again the next day.

Cultivate a support network. Working by yourself can be a lonely business so it is imperative that you build up a community of other freelance pals. This can either be in a co-working space, if you have one, online or formulated from people you meet networking. If you have a number of friends who work freelance, then forming a WhatsApp group in which you can bounce ideas off each other or moan about companies failing to pay you on time can be such a source of comfort and sanity.

KAIZEN AND CAREER CHANGE

Making a change when you have been slogging away on the same career path for ages can be a scary and daunting prospect. It can seem like too much of a leap into the unknown when you are in a stable job with a regular income, even if your job doesn't feel right for you. Most people also don't have the luxury of being able to take a drop in wages in order to start again at the bottom of another career ladder. So this is where an incremental approach to change can be highly beneficial. Having a long-term goal of changing career and working towards it gradually can mean that you can test out whether you like your new chosen career first, perhaps without having to take much of a financial hit in order to do so, and consequently it won't feel quite as scary.

You might not have a clear idea of what your dream career is, but it could be that you have a vague sense that you are unhappy in your current role but are not sure what you really want to change. In this instance, it is best to take a step back and take stock. Write down a list of positives and negatives about your current role.

Which parts of the job do you like doing and which parts do you hate? For example: meeting people, being proactive, negotiating, putting together a really neat spreadsheet, working in a team, working alone, producing events, talking on the phone, travelling, networking, designing things, etc.

Have a think about your strengths and weaknesses For example: caring, being good with new people, decision maker, can make PowerPoints look pretty, struggle with confrontation, not a team player, attention to detail. . .

What about your current work environment? Do you like working in an office? Or do you want to work outside more? Is it too busy or too quiet? Do you come into contact with enough people or too many people? Do you get to use your brain enough? Is it stressful?

Once you have a list of likes and dislikes, and strengths and weaknesses, have a think about which careers might suit you.

Again, friends and family can be very useful in helping with this or else lots of regions operate careers advisory services. Start to collate a list of the positives that you have to offer and any transferable skills that would be useful for your new career path.

It then isn't about making giant leaps to change careers but doing small little things to take you in the right direction. These things might not seem huge on paper but knowing that you are working towards a meaningful goal will motivate you to keep going. Some ideas for small steps you can take to start to explore a career change include:

Talk to your current work. Is there any useful experience you can gain from where you are now? Could it be that you are dissatisfied with your current role and believe that there is a more suitable role within your organization? Or are there at certain skills you need for your dream career that you could learn in your current workplace (the bonus being that you wouldn't have to pay for an expensive training course!)?

Have a conversation with someone who does the role. Before throwing in the towel with your current job, scope out your dream role and really contemplate whether you have what it takes and if it will make you happy. Spending seven years training to be an architect before realizing that the job is just as unfulfilling as your last one will be time badly spent. Ask your friends to see if they know anybody doing the role you are interested in, or approach people who do the role on social media. Most people are happy to give up their time for a coffee or a chat over the phone or email. Otherwise you could seek out podcasts or online interviews to find out more.

First Kaizen Step: research your dream job for an hour.

Try out your new career for a day. Shadow somebody for a day to learn what the nuts and bolts of the job are and see whether you would enjoy it. It might use up one of your holiday days from work, but it is worth it in the long run if it means that you can learn something valuable. If you are looking to move into the charity sector or something to do with the arts, are there any organisations that you can volunteer with to get some invaluable experience?

Look into training. If there are certain skills that your new career requires then research the training options. It could be that this is something you can do in the evening or at weekends, which would mean that you can start working towards your new career while still being paid the salary from your existing job. Don't forget the growing number of online courses that you can do remotely as well.

Get networking. See if there are any industry events that you can gatecrash and keep abreast of newsletters and publications. Say 'yes' to invites and try to meet as many people in the industry as possible. You never know where a chance meeting might lead.

Get your finances in order. If you will have to take a pay cut to change careers, then do an honest analysis of whether you can afford it. Could you ask a friend or family member to help and make a plan to pay them back? Or can you cultivate any 'side hustles' to keep your finances ticking over in the interim? Side hustles are ways of bringing in supplementary income and can be anything from selling some items on eBay, putting your crafts up on Etsy or similar sites, tutoring a student for their exams, dog walking, babysitting or teaching an exercise class. My friend started running a regular Zumba class in her neighbourhood and made enough money to quit her job and relocate to work in a different country.

MEDIUM- AND LONG-TERM GOALS

Changing career can use up a lot of time and energy, so make sure that you are mindful of the timeline and don't try to achieve too much at once. Break down the changes you have to make or the skills you have to learn into really small steps, working towards a medium-term goal, so that you aren't overwhelmed by the workload or alteration to your routine.

If you are already working, then voluntary organizations or training courses will usually aim to be as flexible as possible, and don't be afraid of asking for more time or some time off if you need it. If you are finding it tough to juggle an existing job with your efforts to change career then take it as easy on yourself as possible, slow down if you can, and try to keep the reasons why you wanted a change at the forefront of your mind to keep you motivated. Make some short-term and medium-term goals to get you to the long-term goal of getting your dream job. Invite others to support you and remind you of these reasons too!

KAIZEN AND STUDYING

Whether you are completing exams at school, off to university for the first time, taking a break from your career to study or trying to balance part-time study with work, studying can be extremely stressful. The 'lazy student' stereotype doesn't account for the late nights, the sheer brain power and energy you need, the disruption to your routine and the stress that exams can induce. And in an era when walking out of your studies straight into your dream job is far from guaranteed, the pressure to achieve the best results is even more intense. Recent reports have cited a sharp increase in first-year university students reporting mental health problems, and there has been a trebling of UK students dropping out of university with mental health conditions in the past ten years.[30]

Moving to an entirely new city for the first time or trying to fit lectures and library time around an already-busy job means that other parts of life might be neglected – sleep, diet and exercise routine (ironically, the very things that would probably help to reduce stress levels!). If this is sounding even vaguely familiar, then introducing a few of these habits could be hugely beneficial:

Discover how you work best. Different studying techniques will work for different people. You may have a friend who likes to write out the entirety of the textbook in green pen and try to memorize

it, while you remember things best if the information is in a pretty picture. Find out what works for you and don't try to mimic other people. It may be that you like to work in complete silence or that you remember information better when you are listening to hardcore metal music. Building your study routine around the way that you work best will maximize your time and energy.

Manage your time around how you work most effectively. If you can sit in a library for twelve hours straight without completely losing your mind, then good for you! For the rest of us, working in smaller bursts and taking regular breaks will be far more effective. Think about whether you work better first thing in the morning or whether you are more productive in the afternoon, and fit your routine around that. If you are a morning person, get up early to study but then give yourself the afternoon off. If you are trying to fit studying around paid work, make sure that you allot enough time to your studies and that you aren't trying to cram in too much when you are tired.

Take breaks! It can be easy to just plough on. But taking five minutes out of each hour to get some fresh air or drink water does wonders for motivation and concentration.

Do a little bit every day. This has been a hard lesson for me to learn, but taking a small amount out of each day to study is far better and less stressful than trying to cram it all in at the very last minute. Think of inventive ways that you can manage to do a little bit of studying each day, perhaps even on the bus in the morning.

Prioritize. Be honest about your weaknesses and focus on those first, not on the easy stuff. For example, if you are learning a language and hate revising verb endings, then get this out of the way before practising something that comes easier to you, like conversation.

Keep track of every reference. Make a note of every page number or journal reference as you go along, as it is a total pain in the arse to have to go back through and find everything again. It might seem tedious at the time, but you will thank yourself at the end when you have mountains of footnotes to write.

Study in a stimulating space. Rather than having one really boring wall that you stare at, try mixing up your study environment every so often. Having a different background will stimulate your brain. If you find it useful working with others, set up a study group with people on your course to break up the tedium of having to revise by yourself.

Keep your goal in mind. When you are in the midst of revision or essay-writing hell, it can be easy to forget why you are doing it in the first place. Writing reminders on sticky notes in your study space or changing your computer background to a picture of your goal will remind you why you are doing it. If you want to become a doctor, then hang a stethoscope in your eyeline to keep reminding yourself of what lies ahead.

Keep track of your progress. It can be hard to see any sort of light at the end of the tunnel when you are in the middle of essay writing and revision. Try keeping a log of everything that you do each day – whether it is your word count for an essay or the various books that you have read – so that you can look back and appreciate how hard you have worked.

Plan your day. Rather than looking at the day as an open-ended amount of time in which you have to cram in as much as possible, set yourself small achievable goals at the beginning of each day. It might not be that you achieve them all every single day, but having some focus to your time is a far better tactic than trying to just blast all of the work in a kamikaze fashion.

Reward yourself when it is over. If you can afford it, plan a short weekend break or treat yourself to something that you've wanted for ages. Knowing that there is a Turkish massage or a killer pair of boots waiting at the end of it all will help to keep you motivated.

LOOK AFTER YOURSELF

It can be easy to neglect your mental and physical health when you are studying. Rather than taking an hour out of your evening to cook something healthy, you might often feel like grabbing something on the go and using the extra time for your work. But busy and stressful periods are actually the time when your body needs you to look after it the most. It is imperative to stay healthy – and it will help to improve your concentration and energy levels too. Double win! Here are a few very small ways that you can continue to keep up good habits while you are studying:

Don't overdo the caffeine! It can be easy to rely heavily on coffee when you are studying, but too much caffeine will dehydrate you and cause energy crashes. Invest in a reusable bottle and set an alarm on your phone to refill it with water every two hours or so. The break from the books or screen will do your brain good too.

Keep to a sleep routine. It can be tempting to 'pull an all-nighter' when you have loads of work to do, but can you realistically do your best work at 3am? Try to keep to as regular a sleep routine as possible and get at least seven to eight hours per night.

Stay clear of the junk. A friend at university (who shall remain nameless) often used to eat kebab meat shaved onto pizza, with extra cheese on top. Don't do this. Your body will appreciate it a lot more if you consume foods that contain some basic nutrients during stressful periods. Batch-cooking something healthy at the weekend that you can then eat during the week will save you money in the long run and you will feel so much better for it.

> *First Kaizen step: get all of your course mates together and plan a super-healthy meal to eat.*

Move your body. Spending time on exercise might seem like the last thing you should do, but stretching your limbs and moving about does wonders for stress and energy levels. If you don't have time to go to an exercise class, try a short yoga video when you first wake up.

Practise mindfulness and breathing exercises. Devoting even ten minutes a day to concentrating on your breath and releasing the tension in your body will have a huge de-stressing effect.

> *First Kaizen step: practise the Five-minute lunch-break meditation exercise on page 133.*

お金

okane : money

●●●●○○○○

MONEY | OKANE

The man who moves a mountain begins by carrying away small stones – Confucius

It almost goes without saying that money is a major source of anxiety for a lot of people, especially in current times when wages are stagnating in most places and not growing in line with inflation or the costs of goods and services. Even if you are earning a decent wage or are lucky enough to get help from your family or partner, it can still be a struggle to budget for everything that you need on a day-to-day basis. That's before you even get to saving up for things in the future – whether that's a deposit on a flat or house of your own, a car or going on holiday every so often. I have touched on ideas for ways to change careers in the previous chapter and there are some ideas for side hustles on page 153, but in this chapter we are going to concentrate on spending and saving habits.

Lots of people say that they struggle to change their spending habits. It's easy to think every so often 'oh, well I'm just not going to spend any money this week,' but that is an impossible aim because unless you go and live 'off grid' in a hut in the wilderness somewhere, you need to spend money to be able to survive on a daily basis. There might be some people who can go 'cold turkey' and really deprive themselves of anything but essential items, but I am definitely not one of them and nor are most of the people in my life!

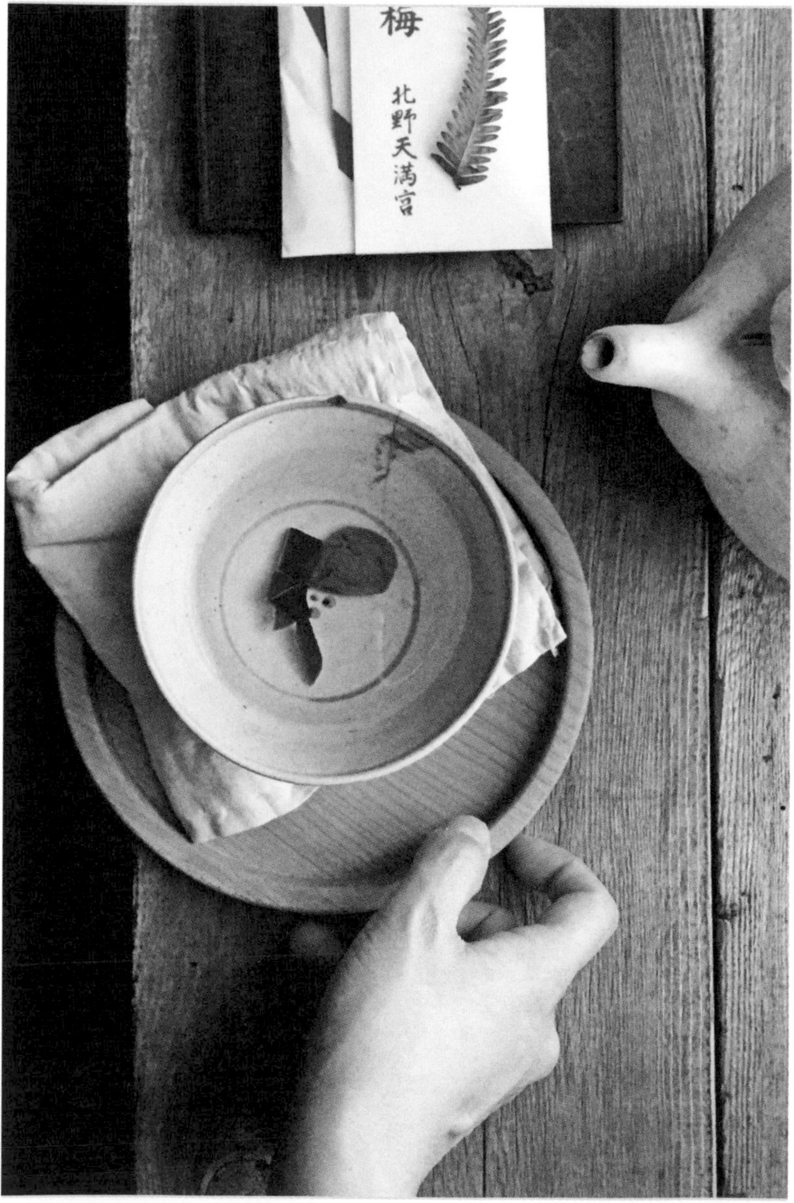
梅
北野天満宮

One of the reasons it can be so hard to change our spending habits is because they are deeply cemented into our daily routine, and the action of spending money also has an emotional aspect to it. I am one of those people who goes shopping – either online or in the real world – when I'm feeling bored, stressed or unhappy about something. I also shop when I'm happy and feeling celebratory, and I have a tendency to go overboard and beyond my means. I have never got into serious debt but there are lots of ways that I know I could be better, and I'm trying to transform my attitude towards money.

If you are in debt and find it impossible to not be in your overdraft at the end of each month or to save any money whatsoever, then it can seem like an insurmountable task to actually make a difference to your situation. This is where starting very small and not trying to change everything at once can be very effective. I think it's useful to see this section not only as a resource for ways in which you can alter bad spending habits, but also for ways in which you can reframe money in a more positive light, as something you can have control over by creating good saving habits.

As with all of the other sections in this book, the first stage of the process is going to be about taking a step back, analysing your current habits and thinking about your goals. We will then go on to look at ideas for small alterations you can make in order to change bad spending habits. Everybody's situation will be different, but I hope that there will be at least one small, relevant change that you can make which will spur you on to make other changes. The final part will then take a more positive attitude towards your finances and discuss ideas for ways you can start to save money. And, obviously, the two concepts are interlinked: if you change your bad spending habits then you are more likely to be able to save more money!

'WHY AM I SO BAD WITH MONEY?'

The first thing to do is to stop beating yourself up, whatever your situation. Life can be shit sometimes and spending money on treats or ways to make life easier and more convenient when you're working hard and are tired is what *everybody* does. And you should still do this occasionally! This section isn't about depriving yourself of any fun whatsoever but rather it is about altering your mindset so that you are more mindful of where your money is going, what your triggers are for spending, and thinking of ways that you can transform your habits for the better. It's not about stopping spending altogether.

HOW TO TRACK YOUR SPENDING

Start by breaking your spending down into essential and non-essential items. There are some debit-card apps which do this job for you and categorize everything that you spend on the card, and there are other apps available where you can log your spending yourself. But this probably won't take into account the money you are spending on rent/mortgage, bills, insurance and other essential items.

Depending on whether you are a spreadsheet or paper person, go with what works best for you. You can either go through the previous month's spending or track your spending as it goes along over the next month. If you are already doing a bullet journal (see page 56), then add a money-tracking section to your monthly pages or dedicate a whole separate journal to it. Or, if you prefer to track your spending electronically, then set up a spreadsheet. In order to make sure you remember to fill this in, try to tack it on to one of your other habits. For example, each Friday morning fill it in when you have your morning coffee. You don't have to go into minutiae but it helps to have a record of your bills and non-essential spending.

KAKEIBO, THE JAPANESE METHOD OF SAVING MONEY

Kakeibo (kah-keh-boh) translates as 'household financial ledger' and was a method invented in 1904 by a Japanese woman called Hani Motoko, notable for being Japan's first female journalist. It is essentially a journaling method, which she invented to help Japanese

women at the time keep on top of their finances, something which she thought was essential for general happiness. Similar to how a bullet journal works, the idea is to keep a ledger of everything that is incoming and outgoing. Motoko emphasized the importance of physically writing it down as a way to mindfully process what you have to spend each month. She encouraged having a 'check in' with the ledger every day to analyse how your spending is progressing, and also taking stock at the end of each month to help you decide which goals to concentrate on in the following month.

ESSENTIAL SPENDING

Once you have this information in front of you, take a step back and really analyse your spending by category. Think about essential spending first – the items you need to survive:

⊙ Housing costs – rent or mortgage
⊙ Utilities – gas and/or electric, phone and internet bills, insurance
⊙ Transport – petrol, travelcard, insurance, tax, any repairs
⊙ Student loan or other debt repayment
⊙ Groceries
⊙ Childcare costs
⊙ Pet costs – food, vet bills, insurance, doggy daycare
⊙ Medical costs – prescriptions, essential toiletries

Most of these costs will be unavoidable (unless you give away your dog or child!), but do have a think if there is a way that you can reduce any of them:

Change supplier. Most utility companies rely on the fact that most people are too lazy to change to a competitor, but it can save lots of money. There are now companies you can give your utility details to and they do the hard work of finding you a new, lower-cost contract.

Make your home more energy-efficient. Lots of governments are now subsidizing various ways to make homes greener and more efficient. Whether that is adding solar panels to your roof, adding insulation to attic spaces or walls, or smaller initiatives like water-saving showers and LED lightbulbs. Think of a few ways that you could make your home more efficient and bring down bills, whether that is turning the heating down a few degrees and wearing an extra layer or making sure that you don't leave your phone charger plugged in all day because you're too lazy to unplug it. If you are tracking your bills, you will quickly see what a big difference these very small changes will make to your energy consumption – and therefore the cost!

Negotiate a new phone/internet contract. Make sure you note down when it is a month before your current contract runs out as this is the time when companies are desperate to retain you as a customer and you can negotiate good deals. Research if any competitors are offering a better deal than the one you are currently on and ask your current supplier to match it. If they won't, then leave. If you like your handset and don't need an upgrade, then SIM-only contracts are far cheaper.

Shop smart and mindfully. Everybody would love to have the time and money to waltz into their local delicatessen every few days and stock up on delicious artisan produce. But most people are frazzled after work and walking like zombies around their local supermarket, desperately trying to cobble together a meal. Supermarkets are famously designed to trick us into spending more money; they have the cheap fruit and veg items near the entrance to encourage us to spend more later, and they put pricier products on the right-hand side of the aisles, as this is the side that we tend to look at first. An easy way to save time and money is to plan your meals properly, take a shopping list with you and do one big shop a week. There are also online tools you can use that store your shopping list, and then tell you which supermarket will offer you the best deals that week.

CULTURE AND ENTERTAINMENT

And now it is time to move on to the harder-to-analyse and more emotional side of your spending: the entertainment and non-essential items!

First, break down the cultural items, holidays and any entertainment or activities that you have spent money on this month, including:

- ⊙ Books, newspapers, magazines
- ⊙ Entertainment subscriptions – TV/film/sport/music-streaming services
- ⊙ Tickets – sport, theatre, cinema, comedy, art shows, gigs, experiences
- ⊙ Gym membership, exercise classes
- ⊙ Holidays or weekends away – accommodation, flights, trains, spending money
- ⊙ Birthday parties, weddings, hen/stag dos
- ⊙ Haircuts and beauty appointments

Have a think about these purchases and the motivation behind your decision to spend money on them. Questions to ask yourself might be:

Were they worthwhile?
Did they provide an opportunity for you to have fun with your partner/friends/family?
Can you afford them? Or did you overspend?
Are there any ways you could have cut costs?

You will probably find that for most of the items on this list you will have felt a sense of satisfaction from buying them because they offered you a fun experience with your loved ones, they were culturally enriching or they helped you to relax. You should budget some 'fun money' into your spending plan, otherwise you might abandon your spending goals. The Kaizen approach to spending is about being mindful of what you are spending and making the right choices to ensure that you live within your means.

If you do feel like you are spending too much money, have a think about whether there is any way you can reduce your outgoings.

Talk to your friends! I have often spent money that I didn't have on various hen dos and weddings when I could have just gone for less time or done it in a cheaper way. If you are worried about spending money on a big event, then have a quiet word with your friend and see if there is a way you can do it more cheaply. They will definitely understand – and if they don't then they probably aren't worth being friends with!

Change or cancel your entertainment package. Do you really need subscriptions to two different film-streaming services *and* your monthly unlimited-film cinema ticket? Are you paying for a service that you don't use?

Think about your usage. If you are paying for a gym membership or for every individual yoga class, be honest about whether you are getting value for money. Could you buy classes in bulk and save money?

DIY! Getting a regular massage or nail appointment can be a very enjoyable luxury. But if you can't afford it then have a think about alternatives: can you get your friend to do your nails? Or can you wax your legs yourself? It might not be quite the same as being in a professional salon, but you will save oodles of money.

NON-ESSENTIALS

Think about the other non-essential items – the things you probably buy on impulse and might not necessarily need, such as clothes and shoes, accessories, homeware, flowers and plants, make-up, meals out, takeaways, coffee, snacks.

Lots of these things might not necessarily be entirely frivolous purchases. If it's cold then you need a winter coat, or if you are feeling really glum then some flowers are a fairly inexpensive way to cheer yourself up. This isn't meant to be encouraging you to cut all joy out of your life, but we turn to these kinds of things when in need of a quick 'spending fix'. While you are tracking your spending, try asking yourself the following questions when considering purchasing one of these items:

Do I need this? Will it be useful and does it make me feel excited?
Is there an obvious home for it where I live?
Being truly honest with myself, how do I feel about buying it? Happy, excited, indifferent?
If it's an item of clothing, or shoes or accessories: can I think of at least three existing items in my wardrobe with which I could wear this?
What is my emotional state in general today? Am I stressed, celebratory, feeling bad about myself, calm?

From analysing your responses to the questions above, you can start to identify any emotional triggers to your spending. It's a good idea to explore if there are any environmental triggers too. For example, if you made a purchase, then ask yourself the following questions.

Was I killing time?
Did I buy the item because I read about it or received a marketing email about it?
Was I intending to spend money on this item before I went to the shops or opened the link in my browser?

Think about how you feel about having spent the money:

Do I feel happy with my purchase?
Do I regret it?
Was I in a frenzy when I bought it?
Will I find the purchase useful?
Am I focusing on quantity over quality?
And am I spending in the most ethical, sustainable and environmentally friendly way?

A lot of these purchases will be justified and essential, but below are ideas for small ways in which you can modify your behaviour to ensure you spend more mindfully:

Leave the item for twenty-four hours. This highlights whether you genuinely want or need it. If you are still thinking about the item the next day and can afford it, then make the purchase. I promise you will feel a greater sense of satisfaction about the decision.

Watch out for sales. I always go a bit crazy when I see a sale sign. But it often means that I end up spending money on items that I don't really need or use. For each item that you have in your basket during a sale, ask yourself whether you would buy it if it were full price.

Check your bank balance regularly. I used to be one of those people who would cross their fingers that a purchase would go through when it got to the last week of the month. I never had any idea how much money I had and buried my head in the sand until I could brave looking at my balance once I got paid. Checking your balance helps to lower your anxiety levels because you feel more in control and it really brings into focus how much money you have to spend. I make a habit of checking my banking app when I first get to my desk in the morning. It's a scary habit to try at first but does wonders for worry levels.

Spend in cash. Physically handing over cash rather than just mindlessly tapping your card makes you more conscious of what you are spending, and you will find it easier to budget.

> *First Kaizen step: try taking out a set amount of cash to use for the week and only spending what you have. Notice if it feels different to spend in this way.*

Put reminders in your wallet. My friend attached a sticker to her credit card which bluntly said, 'DO YOU NEED THIS? REALLY?!' and it meant that she always had a prompt whenever she was about to spend money. Anything which encourages you to pause and take a breath before making a purchase is going to be beneficial.

> *First Kaizen step: attach a note to your wallet for a week and see if it breaks the automaticity of reaching for your card and buying something.*

Change the environments that cause you to spend. If you notice that you often spend money after clicking on emails from different brands or seeing pictures of influencers wearing a brand on Instagram, then unfollow or unsubscribe. Or if you buy clothes or make-up when you have time to kill, try using this time to do another activity instead, such as having a walk in the park.

Be thrifty. Are you an avid reader who doesn't belong to a library? Do you mend your clothes when they have holes in them or leave them at the back of your wardrobe? Do you sew buttons back on? Do you freeze food, such as bread, herbs and veggies that you won't have a chance to eat before their sell-by date?

Keep reminders of payment deadlines. I have a friend who has had her car impounded three (three!) times because she forgot to renew her car tax. Don't be like her. If you are using a journal, then make sure to write down payment deadlines for your credit card, your bills and annoying yearly payments that are easy to forget (like car tax!).

Everybody will occasionally want to treat themselves. This is fine and to be encouraged! This exercise is more about cutting out those purchases that might give you a temporary boost but that you either forget about five minutes later or don't use. It's about encouraging you to pause and take a breath before making a decision to spend money on something that you don't need. Nobody is perfect and you probably won't remember to do this every time, but even being slightly more mindful of the way that you are spending your money will make a huge difference – and hopefully the small changes and savings you make will start to have a cumulative effect on your bank balance and help you to save money for a rainy day.

HOW CAN I GO SAVE MORE MONEY?

The acts of mindfully spending and saving are very much interlinked, as you will find that the more you spend wisely, the more money you have left over to save. But there are also proactive ideas to save more:

Have a separate savings account. It sounds hugely obvious but if the money is in your current account then you will feel more inclined to spend it. Open a savings account and transfer an amount into it at the beginning of the month so that you know that you can't touch it. Or if you have money left before payday – however small an amount – transfer it over to the savings account. Savings accounts pay interest, too, so your efforts to open another account will pay off.

Use savings apps. There are now several mobile apps that will do the saving for you automatically. They analyse the amount you are spending each week, then transfer over a balance that it thinks you can afford to a savings account, or it will round up whatever you are spending to the nearest pound/euro/dollar then transfer over the rest. You barely notice that you are saving because the amounts are so small, but they soon build up and you can usually transfer the money back right away if you need to.

Have a coin jar. This may sound a bit old-school, but most people will have some loose change hanging around their house. If you keep it to one side and save it up you can then take it along to the bank to be paid directly into your account. Lots of supermarkets also have machines that will count it for you and pay you the amount in larger denominations for the price of a small commission.

> **First Kaizen step:** *get into the habit of emptying all of the coins in your purse or wallet into a jar at the end of the week and watch it build up.*

Have reminders of what you are saving for. It is good to remind yourself of whatever goal it is that you are saving towards to keep up your motivation. Why not have a picture of the holiday destination you want to go to as your computer background?

Let a friend or partner hold you accountable for your spending and saving. If you involve another person in your spending and saving goals, then you are far more likely to want to stick to them. Being transparent with somebody else encourages you to be transparent with yourself.

ie : home

●●●●●○○○

HOME | IE

If dust piles up it becomes a mountain – Japanese proverb

The main thing that I have taken away from living in and visiting Japanese homes is the close attention paid to how space is used. Because it is limited, especially in cities, every inch of the room is used, and many rooms serve as multi-functional spaces.

I stayed in a house in Hiroshima that had just one room for a living and sleeping space, with a futon bed kept in a nearby cupboard to roll out at night to sleep on. Although Japan is the size of California, it has a population of 89.2 million compared to California's 37.3 million, and around 73 per cent of its land is mountainous. This means that most of the population inhabits the remaining 27 per cent of space, and as such, urban areas are very densely populated, with people living in very close proximity to each other. The result of this is that people are used to living in smaller spaces and they work hard to ensure that the space is utilized to its full effect. Functionality and simple minimalism are key components of Japanese design – and ones which have been successfully exported to the West, with Japanese shops like Muji and Uniqlo popularizing a very simple and practical aesthetic.

The geological make-up of Japan has also affected the design of houses themselves and the materials used to build them. Because

of its location and its mountainous terrain, Japan is prone to natural disasters, such as earthquakes, typhoons and tsunamis. This has meant that, traditionally, Japanese homes have been made from natural materials like wood, clay and concrete; materials which are easy to replace and rebuild if the house has to be reconstructed after a natural disaster. It was also very hard to transport heavier materials before the modern road system, hence the preference for lighter materials such as wood.

Unlike in the West, where homes tend to be built from stone or brick and can last for hundreds of years, traditionally, Japanese homes tend to have a shorter lifespan and there is less of a focus on permanence. Even nowadays, when the design of Japanese homes has developed and modern houses are built to withstand earthquakes and extreme weather, the average lifespan of a house is still between twenty and thirty years, and unlike the West,[31] the value of homes depreciate over time, with houses typically demolished if the occupant moves on or dies, and a new house built in its place.

The focus on natural materials and functionality is still prevalent in Japanese homes today, with many modern homes continuing to use some of the traditional methods of design and style of furniture. Rooms in the traditional Japanese style always contain tatami mats, which are yellow-green mats made from rice straw and soft rush that have been plaited, pressed and edged with fabric. Tatami mats are used in multiples to cover the whole floor of a room. They also serve as a unit of measurement – for example, *cha no yu*, the Japanese tea ceremony, would take place in a space the size of two tatami mats. The rooms are then divided by *fusuma*, vertical paper-covered rectangular panels, which can be moved to reshape the room to

whatever purpose it is needed for. Historically, these would be painted with scenes from nature, whether that is mountains, trees, flowers or animals. As well as *fusuma*, rooms are also divided by *shōji*, similar-sized panels covered with translucent paper to allow light to pass through between rooms. Traditionally, the outside walls of houses would also be made up of these moveable panels so that there was less of a delineation between the outside garden and the interior. To this day, many Japanese homes still use tatami mats as their floor coverings and use panels to help to delineate the space.

This sense of transience and portability is also reflected in the furnishings and appliances in the house. Furniture is often designed to be stacked or be easily moved around. Rather than having a permanent sofa, there might be floor cushions or chairs which can be moved to suit whatever purpose. Traditionally, Japanese people slept on futons on the floor, which could be rolled up during the day to create more space, and this is the way that some people still choose to sleep. Kitchen equipment and appliances are often cleverly designed so that they can be stacked or stored easily – the most famous export being the bento style of lunchbox.

KAIZEN AND THE HOME

So how does this all relate to Kaizen and your habits? Well, spending time in a country that offers alternative designs for homes and a different emphasis on what their function should be and their permanence – or lack of – has made me interrogate what I want from my living space. I am keen to improve my tidying habits and to create a relaxing living space that works for me. In Japan, I only had a couple of suitcases of possessions (my friends doubted that I would survive with so little when I left England!) and it showed me how you can totally get by with the bare minimum of items. Before I went away, I used to fill every surface that I had with items of make-up or jewellery, and my wardrobe was often bulging with clothes that I didn't actually wear. Being more restricted made me vow to embrace minimalism and donate items that I don't need.

If you are tired from work or feeling overwhelmed and mentally drained by the outside world, then dedicating time to improving your living space can seem like a chore. Newspapers, magazine articles, television programmes and lifestyle bloggers often peddle expensive and aspirational improvements or furnishings for your home, which can make having a comfortable living space feel out of reach. And this is before we even consider the stresses that we have little control over, such as inconsiderate housemates or children who leave their toys everywhere! It can feel like an uphill battle to keep everything in order before you even stop to think if it is a pleasant and welcoming space.

I always felt that tidying was a hugely time-consuming and boring task that I was never able to get on top of. But living in such small spaces in Japan transformed my attitude to tidying and made me want to change my habits. I have really noticed the difference it has made to my anxiety levels and sleep quality as well; the messiness of my living space always correlates to my state of mind and tidying it helps me to feel better.

For fellow tidying-phobes and anybody who wants to change their living space, making a small effort each day to improve your environment can make a huge cumulative difference. Rather than feeling like you have to tackle everything all at once, breaking it down into very small chunks makes it all seem far more manageable.

TAKE STOCK

Before doing anything at all, take some time to step back and really look at how you are using your living space. If you live with other people, whether that is family or housemates, choose just one room in the house (ideally the one that you spend the most time in or your favourite room) and analyse how you feel about the room.

Is there clutter?
Does everything have a home?
Do you have enough storage?
Do you need everything?
How does the room make you feel? Calm/happy/stressed/anxious?
Is it clean?
Does anything need fixing?
Do you like the furnishings?

Make a list of things that could be improved/cleaned/fixed/tidied and next to each item, write a small thing you can do towards making that improvement. And then note how it will make you feel to make that change.

FOR EXAMPLE

I haven't hung up my clothes for ages and I have a 'floor-drobe' instead of a wardrobe.

- *Sort out the pile into clean and dirty clothes and collate the clean clothes by type of clothing.*
- *It would give me more floor space and I would feel less stressed.*

Two of the lightbulbs have gone in the bathroom and I haven't changed them because I can't reach the fitting.

- *Buy some lightbulbs and ask a friend to fix them.*
- *I will have a lovely, light bathroom that will feel more uplifting.*

Depending on how much time you have, make a commitment to implementing one of these changes either every day for a week, or one on each day of the weekend if you are busy during the week. They should be small things that take no more than ten minutes of your time. Lots of other ideas for tidying methods and ways to improve your space are in the next section.

Your home should be a sanctuary from the outside world, not another source of stress! Focus your attention on improving just one room and see the effect it has on your mental state and how you feel about your home. It may spur you on to want to tackle more rooms in the house. And if you live with others, don't take all of the burden on yourself; involve your partner, your children and your friends. A stress-free home will benefit them as much as you.

TIDYING TECHNIQUES

Japanese tidying techniques have been popularized recently by Marie Kondo's KonMari method, which has also inspired many other books, online videos and magazine articles devoted to tidying. Tidying is having a moment. But in Japan, tidying and cleaning techniques are instilled in people from a young age. Schools have a practice called *gakko soji* (school cleansing), which encourages pupils to take responsibility for keeping classrooms tidy. Every day, often after lunchtime, students tidy and clean the classroom for twenty minutes before getting back to their studies, often to fun music played over the tannoy system. The extent to which students clean varies between schools and different age groups, but the root of the practice comes from Shinto teachings, where monks devote time to cleaning the temple each day and at the end of the year practise *susu-harai* (house cleaning), which is like a huge spring clean.

Hardly anybody will have the time or energy to commit to a big clean-up every day, but using Kaizen methods to slowly make changes to your environment will encourage you to persevere with creating a calming and functional living space. Even something as small as making sure that you hang up your clothes in the wardrobe before going to bed means that you wake up feeling more relaxed.

Take stock of what you own, what matters to you and what you regularly use. The idea isn't to throw away absolutely all of your possessions and live like a Buddhist monk (unless you wish to). The aim is to have a designated space for everything rather than having random drawers or cupboards overloaded with stuff that you're keeping 'for a rainy day' but will never actually use.

CLOTHES

Do an honest analysis of the clothes in your drawers and wardrobe. Do you wear everything? Are you are keeping hold of items in the hope that you might 'one day fit into them'? Having everything in one visible pile highlights how much you have, what you like, and the items that are surplus to requirements.

> *First Kaizen step: choose a wardrobe or chest of drawers and take everything out to create a pile.*

Sort out the pile. For wardrobe items, rehang everything that you regularly wear, with the heaviest items (coats and jackets) on the left and the lighter items to the right (longer items such as dresses, followed by trousers, then skirts, then tops). Repeat this for drawer items that you regularly use, such as t-shirts and jumpers, then put everything that you haven't worn in the last year in a pile. If they have tags on, be honest with yourself about whether you need or like the item. For the remaining items, do the same thing. If they are clothes that you don't wear often but want to keep because of an emotional attachment, can you find another place to store them, such as under your bed?

Sort out your underwear! Have your knickers or boxers lost their elastic? Are your tights bobbly? Do your socks have holes in them? Do you own bras that don't fit you? Chuck them if they are unusable or send to charity/recycle if they still have wear.

> **First Kaizen step:** *sort through your sock drawer and throw out any socks that aren't in a pair.*

Assess what shoes you have. Do you have any shoes which are slightly too big but that you spent a lot of money on and can't bear to part with? Be honest with yourself about which shoes you actually wear and will wear in the future. Recycle any you don't wear regularly.

Mend holes, broken zips and rips. If you have several items that you never wear because they have imperfections, either recycle these items or mend them. If you are lacking in sewing skills, then ask a family member to help or take them to a local tailor who will mend items cheaply.

> **First Kaizen step:** *set a target of sewing a button back onto an item of clothing by the end of the week.*

Sort out your accessories. Do you have mountains of scarves, endless tote bags, hairbands or sunglasses that don't suit you but that you can't bear to part with? Lay out all of your accessories on the floor and be honest about what you like and actually use. Then make sure that all of the items that you want to keep have a home – supermarkets and home shops often sell cheap wicker baskets which are perfect for keeping them all in one place.

Recycle, recycle, recycle! Once you have decided which items to chuck, try to get rid of them quickly so that you're not tempted to reintroduce them. Sort the pile into:

⊙ Items you can potentially sell on eBay, or on other clothes-selling sites
⊙ Items you can sell at a car boot sale or flea market
⊙ Items you want to donate to charity
⊙ Items you can give to friends or family. Arranging a clothes-swap session once or twice a year can be a really fun way to get rid of your stuff and gain some new items for your wardrobe. One person's trash is another person's treasure, after all.

BOOKS/NEWSPAPERS/MUSIC/DVDS

The Japanese use the term *tsundoku* to describe acquiring books and reading materials which then remain unread. Having a job which means that I often get given books for free means that I am particularly guilty of this one! If you have lots of space in your house and are cultivating a library, then of course don't get rid of your books. But if you feel like you are sometimes overwhelmed by reading material, then having a clear-out can be cathartic.

Be realistic. Are you holding on to books you will probably never read but which look good in your bookcase? Have a think about whether you want your book collection to be representative of what you actually like to read or if it is there to make you look intellectual. (It's fine if it is the latter but remember that it is restricting space for books you actually want to read.)

Give yourself permission to keep favourite books. Do you have a book given to you by a grandparent who is no longer with us or signed by a favourite author? Then, of course, hold on to it. But alter your mindset so that you give yourself permission to have it rather than feeling guilty about the space it takes up.

Throw away old magazines and newspaper supplements. I am guilty of having a 'to be read' pile next to my bed. There are only so many hours in the day to get through everything. Will you ever actually get around to reading through the pile? Recycle, recycle, recycle.

Sort through your music and film collections. Approach these as you did your books. Keep anything of sentimental value and anything which you regularly use, but be realistic about whether you have the space for items that you never listen to or watch.

Sell, sell, sell! The great thing about books and music is that they often have resale value. There are now online companies that will take a job lot of items and give you a price for them (often calculated by scanning the barcodes with your phone). I did this with my books before I went to Japan and made over £100.

PAPERS

Are you guilty of shoving paperwork in a drawer or box and forgetting about it? Sorting it out can transform how tidy your space feels – and how tidy your mind feels.

First, separate out the important stuff. I don't advocate becoming completely paperless. Separate out anything important, such as legal documents, passport, driver's licence, marriage/birth certificates, etc. I bought a pretty box to store these in, but any old shoebox or file will do.

Sort out everything else. Do you really need your old gas bill from 2009? Take all of your other paperwork and sort it into date order. You rarely need to keep copies of any bills older than six months, and most can be downloaded now anyway. Similarly, do you really need the instruction manual for your phone or your oven? Nearly every manual can be found online these days too, and all of the information can be searched. Throw away or shred.

> *First Kaizen step: each month, set a reminder and spend five minutes sorting out the bills and paperwork at the older end of the date spectrum.*

MISCELLANEOUS ITEMS

This is anything from batteries, skincare, make-up, electronic equipment (such as random chargers), stationery, travel shampoo and a sewing kit to household items like sticky tape, wrapping paper, string, screwdrivers and cleaning products. Most of these will be things either that you take pleasure from or that are useful. But there are probably also lots which are surplus to requirements.

> *First Kaizen step: choose one drawer of miscellaneous stuff and sort through it.*

Recycle old batteries and electrical equipment. Check if batteries actually work and recycle them if not. And do you know what every single wire or charger does in your drawer? If not, chuck it! Are you really going to mend that broken pair of hair straighteners? Be honest with yourself.

Do an inventory of your toiletries and make-up. Do you have an expensive make-up that doesn't suit you or half-used moisturizers that make you break out? If the product is new, then there are several charities that will accept make-up and toiletries. Otherwise, do you have a friend or family member who might use it more?

PLATES + DISHES

Sort through stationery, art supplies and wrapping paper. Does everything still work and do you use it? Does it all have a home? Find one if not. Lots of schools, churches and local nurseries will accept donations of art equipment.

Do you need all of your travel accessories? Are you holding on to some ear plugs that you got free on a flight in case you might ever need them? Or half-filled miniature shampoo bottles? If you are honestly ever going to use them then find a home for them, otherwise get rid.

Be honest with yourself about sports equipment! Are you holding on to an old exercise bike because you plan to one day use it again? Do you have a yoga mat covered in dust? Do you have a pair of arm weights under your bed that you have never actually used? If you want to keep the items, then set yourself a monthly target to use them – and if you don't, sell or recycle them. They will just sit there making you feel guilty otherwise.

SENTIMENTAL ITEMS

Items with sentimental value can often be the toughest to sort through. These can be anything from photos, ornaments and trinkets to jewellery that you have inherited, crockery, clothes, holiday souvenirs, old children's books or toys and pieces of furniture. The point isn't to get rid of everything that you feel attached to, but to decide, rationally, if you really need or want them. The following prompts can help:

Do you use it? If so, great!

If not, do you get pleasure from owning the item? Everything you own should make you feel good. If an item is making you feel upset or guilty then give yourself permission to get rid of it.

Does it have a clear place that it lives in your home? If it doesn't have a natural place, is it surplus to requirements?

If you want to keep it, is there a better way to store it? For example: vacuum-packed, in a cool dry place like the loft? Or can you give it to a friend or family member for safekeeping?

Are you hanging on to stuff from family members because you feel like you have to? Remember that you can ditch the clutter without ditching the memories of that person.

Can you digitize the memory instead? Rather than keeping boxes and boxes of old photos which you rarely look at, can you digitize them? (Lots of photo shops will do this for you.) Rather than hold on to a printed copy of your dissertation thesis, can you scan it?

Acknowledge your attachment to items. Are you holding on to all of your child's old toys because you can't bear the thought of him growing up? Or the clothing of a relative that doesn't fit you, but which reminds you of a person who you loved? Can you keep one or two special items and part with the rest? Donating to another loving home means you are passing the memory to a positive cause.

Be gentle with yourself. Clearing out sentimental items isn't about removing the memory of that person or time; it is about giving yourself permission to move on and create room for new memories in your life.

IMPROVING YOUR SPACE

Think about small differences you can make to improve the rooms that you live in. One tip that a friend gave to me is to always treat your home as if a loved one is about to visit for the first time. Think of how nice you'd want to make it for them (possibly by having a panicked tidy and a quick change of bedding!) and try to channel that all of the time. You want your home to reflect your personality, and for it to be a haven from the outside world.

We'd all love an unlimited budget and an interior designer who could come up with a 'vision' for our homes. But most of us have to make do with cheap flea-market finds and Sweden's popular budget home store. The media constantly bombards us with pictures of expensive furnishings, but try these small changes that make a huge difference.

Think about lighting and air. Japanese temples are traditionally designed to bring in as much air and light as possible. Getting fresh air into your rooms will make you feel far more energized than breathing in stale, old air. Rather than a big overhead light, invest in lamps and candles to make the space feel cosier and warmer.

Bring the outside inside. In the same way that traditional Japanese homes have moveable walls on the outside to reduce the feeling of divide between interior and garden, think of ways you can introduce the outside into your home. Can you think of ways that you can make your home more seasonal? Research plants that are in season.

Improve your storage solutions. Cheap and attractive boxes and baskets can be found really easily these days and are so useful for keeping all of your small miscellaneous items, such as make-up and chargers, in one place.

> *First Kaizen step: create some pretty storage by covering old shoe boxes in offcuts of wallpaper or wrapping paper; a really inexpensive way to make your storage look attractive.*

Personalize your space. Decorating your home with memories of your life is the easiest and cheapest way to bring your personality into the space and make you feel more at home. Invest in some picture frames and frame your photos and any prints or posters that you own. Lots of charity shops or flea markets have picture frames you can buy for next-to-nothing. Corkboards are also an excellent way to pin up postcards, photos and other mementos that mean something to you.

Introduce some colour. Painting a wall a different colour can have a transformative effect and it doesn't have to cost very much at all. If you have a landlord who won't let you decorate, then invest in some colourful cushion covers, curtains or patterned rugs. Make sure that you keep an eye on eBay, Gumtree, Facebook, Freecycle and other local sites where you can pick up furnishings for free or at very low cost – which has the added bonus of being more environmentally friendly.

Surround yourself with nice smells. Opening your windows regularly and keeping your home clean – especially the carpets and soft furnishings – should eliminate any nasty smells, but introducing good smells into your house can also promote relaxation and make the space feel more pleasant. Use scented candles, buy a reed or oil diffuser, burn incense or buy fresh flowers. Boiling citrus fruit and fresh herbs in water on your stove works as a great natural potpourri, and adding lime or lemon juice to (cold) light bulbs creates a fresh scent when the light is switched on.

The idea is to introduce good habits and small changes so your home feels more like a haven and a place that you want to relax in at the end of the day. It's about assessing your space and then thinking of some small (and cheap!) ways in which you could make it work better for you.

関
係

kankei : relationships

● ● ● ● ● ● ○ ○

RELATIONSHIPS | KANKEI

Friends are known first in hardships – Japanese proverb

Your relationships – whether with a partner, a family member, a friend, a colleague or with yourself – will evolve over time and ebb and flow. A university friendship might look very different when you are in your late thirties and have stressful careers or families of your own. Similarly, a couple who have retired together will discover that their relationship suddenly looks entirely different from how it was when they were both working and not under each other's feet all of the time. Your relationship with your sibling might transform when one of you moves to another town. The way that you feel about yourself as a teenager will be different from your relationship with yourself as an adult. As such, it is important to keep attuned to how you feel about the various relationships in your life. If you are mindful of your relationships and their impact on you, then you are more likely to recognize those relationships that enhance your life and those that are a potentially negative influence.

THE BENEFITS OF RELATIONSHIPS

Humans have always formed bonds with others, and it goes beyond having a cavewoman pal to help collect berries with or a farming mate in the next field with whom you could exchange rice. A feeling

of social connectedness and belonging has been consistently linked to happiness.[32] Good relationships and the support they offer have been shown to reduce our stress levels and promote longer life.[33] You can have the most successful career, infinite amounts of money and good health, but you will still be unhappy if you don't have fulfilling personal relationships. Hundreds of studies have shown the correlation between having good relationships and personal happiness, and psychologists emphasize the quality of your relationships over the quantity of them. It is far better to have a few very meaningful relationships than lots of unsatisfactory ones.

In this day and age, when we are being pulled in so many different directions, the pressure to keep in contact with people – not only in real life but online too – can feel too much at times. It is much easier to stay connected with people, but it also means that there are more people we feel the need to stay connected with. We are expected to quickly respond to every call and message, whether that is a random person on social media or the childminder asking why you dropped off your child wearing a tutu again (answer: she wouldn't wear anything else without screaming and you wanted to make your life easier!). As such, it can be easy to devote your energy to those who demand attention first rather than to those whom you would prefer to give your attention.

DO A RELATIONSHIP INVENTORY

As with all things Kaizen, the first step is to take stock and ask yourself some probing questions about your relationships. Take a piece of paper and divide it into sections, such as family, romantic relationships, friendships, colleagues, etc. For each section, write down the most important people in each category. Rather than feeling like you have to tackle absolutely every relationship in your life at once, initially choose just one or two people who you would like to focus on. This could be because they are the most important person to you, or a person you feel you are drifting away from, or somebody who is going through a tough time. Keep the following questions in the forefront of your mind.

What are the main emotions that the thought of this person evokes? (Happiness, sadness, anxiety, joyfulness, competitiveness, equality, hate, love, hilarity, draining, boosting, burdensome, trusting. . .)

Does this person make an equal effort with me?

Does this person enrich my life by being in it?

When did we last spend quality time together? Do I feel like I want to spend more or less time with them?

Do I feel like my best self when I am with this person?

How has our relationship evolved over time and what has changed (either for the better or worse)?

Do I feel independent enough from this person?

IMPROVING RELATIONSHIPS

Talk! If you are agonizing over the direction that a relationship is taking, it may be that a friend or partner has no idea that you are feeling a little neglected by them or you are sad that you have drifted apart. Or it may be that they have been feeling the same and haven't known how to broach it. Being brave and letting them know how you feel can be transformative. If you feel incapable of doing this face to face, then a wisely worded text or email can do wonders. Conversely, if they react badly or don't seem to care for your feelings, then it is a clear sign that you should extricate yourself from the relationship.

Practise gratitude. Keeping a gratitude journal or diary can remind you to take stock and appreciate those around you. At the end of each day, write down the name of a person who has made you happy and why. Look back on this regularly and appreciate the relationships that you have.

> *First Kaizen step:* keep a gratitude journal for a week and each day write about a person who made your day better.

Let your loved ones know how important they are to you. It is easy to assume that people know how much they mean to you, but that isn't always the case.

> *First Kaizen step:* try choosing one person each week to send a note to – whether that is via text, postcard or email – and tell them why they make you happy, give them a compliment, or tell them that you are thinking of them.

Think of one small act you can do. If your partner is stressed about work, can you make them breakfast in bed? Or if your colleague is upset about something, can you buy them some chocolate from the work vending machine? If your friend is having a hard time, can you go over with a takeaway? Try to do one small act per week and notice how your relationships change.

Celebrate your independence. Try thinking of one activity you can do per week that is just for you and not dependent on anybody else. If you usually go to the cinema with your partner but don't always agree on what to see, then plan a solo trip to see something that you can enjoy without worrying about whether they are hating it or not. It may feel like a contradiction to advocate independence when we're talking about relationships, but having space from others, and especially from your partner, is important for cultivating a relationship with yourself.

Find your tribe. If you are feeling isolated or like you have drifted from some of your friends, then make an effort to find people who have similar interests to you. You could seek out new people locally or online (one of the actual benefits of social media!). And try not to feel guilty about those who you leave behind. Remember that some friends will suit you at a certain time of your life but that you might not have as much in common with them as you get older and your circumstances change. There may be people who fitted your lifestyle when you wanted to go out clubbing every weeknight but who you struggle to talk to now that you don't want to do that any more. Or people who you bonded with over having children at a similar age, but with whom you now share little common ground. Try to accept that this is a natural part of getting older and move on. It is worth spending energy on those who bring you happiness; remember the old adage of quality over quantity!

Reach out to your community. Feeling connected with those around us shouldn't just be limited to your immediate friends and family. Try doing one act a week that will benefit somebody who you don't know. If you have time, then it could be volunteering with a local charity or helping out at a community centre. Or it can be just small one-off gestures, such as buying a coffee for a homeless person and having a chat to them or giving directions to somebody in the street who looks completely lost. You never know what good might happen from these small interactions and putting a bit of kindness back into the world is no bad thing for us all.

DIFFICULT RELATIONSHIPS

There can be some relationships in your life which are unhealthy and can affect you deeply. If there are any people on your relationship inventory who cause you to feel a negative feeling, have a think about why that could be. It may be that the person is going through a difficult time and you don't know the whole story; it could be that they are struggling at work, with their health, or generally feeling bad about themselves and projecting that onto you. They could feel competitive with you or envious of you and are going about it in entirely the wrong way. If the person is important to you, then it is good to address the tension in your relationship before it's too late.

Rather than accosting the person and dealing with the problem in a hot-headed and impulsive manner, it is much better to take a Kaizen approach. Step back and think about where your relationship has gone wrong. Ask yourself the following questions:

Do you know a clear reason or reasons why your relationship has declined?

If so, is there something that you could have done differently? (Try to be as objective as possible here!)

If you're not sure what has gone wrong, what is the best way to find out? Would that person respond to you asking them directly, either in person or in writing? Or would it be better to get help from a mutual friend or relation?

Once you have thought through some of the causes for your relationship breakdown, think of how best to go about building bridges. This will very much depend on the nature of your relationship and what has gone wrong, but remember to be mindful of the following:

- ⊙ *Patience*. You probably won't be able to fix everything at once, so keep in mind your Kaizen small steps and take things slowly. Start out with a coffee or a letter and go from there.

- ⊙ *Clear communication*. Be honest about your feelings and try to convey them as calmly as possible. Make sure that you listen to the other person's point of view too.

- ⊙ *Apologize*. If you have something to apologize for, then do so. Or be ready to accept the other person's apology if they are at fault. Try to avoid the classic 'non-apology', such as 'I'm sorry if you were offended by X.' Be willing to move on once you have apologized.

- ⊙ *Remember the good times and plan for the future*. Keep in mind why that person was so special to you in the first place and why you want to salvage the relationship. Where can you go together in the future?

If you find that the relationship is impossible to salvage, then accept that sometimes it is better to let go of things that are making us miserable. It can be hard to face up to the decline of a relationship, especially when you have invested a lot of energy into it, but as relationships develop as we get older, there might be ones which don't serve us any more. This might be a friend who seemed like the best person in the world at first but who then gradually starts to make comments which make you feel bad about yourself or a colleague who starts off seeming friendly but who then turns on you and makes you feel miserable.

It can be hard to completely cut off contact from some relationships, especially if they are a family member or if you have to see that person every day, but be very mindful of how they make you feel and do try to limit your contact with them as much as you can. Seek support from others to help you with this too, such as another colleague who can change the meeting schedule, or another family member who can keep you away from your annoying uncle at your annual family gathering. Focus your energy on people who boost you and who you come away from feeling positive.

If a person's behaviour ever extends into being abusive or harmful towards you, it is important that you cut off contact with that person altogether if possible. If your partner, a friend or a family member ever treats you disrespectfully or causes you harm – whether that is emotional or physical – then do please seek support to help extricate yourself from the situation.

One kind word can warm three winter months – Japanese proverb

CONNECTING WITH OTHERS

Western society venerates 'self-starters', but it is impossible to be entirely self-reliant all of the time. Being in Japan and experiencing their more collectivist culture really brought home to me the benefits of having a strong support network around you. Although the value system of the younger generation in Japan is slowly

shifting towards more individualism, there is still an emphasis on collectivity and group loyalty, especially with family, friends and colleagues. You can't be expected to do all the heavy lifting when it comes to feeling good about yourself, and it is always helpful to talk to others to get you through tough times. If you are feeling in need of some support, adopt a Kaizen approach and think about how you could build up a better network around you.

Reach out online to find your tribe. Thankfully, one of the good things about social media is that it is easy to access those who have similar interests to you. (Try searching hashtags on Instagram or finding groups on Facebook.) If you are finding it hard to meet people who you connect with in real life, then seeking them out online can make you feel less isolated. Some people might find it easier to open up to others online too.

> *First Kaizen step: find five new social media accounts that you wish to follow or send a message to somebody who you already follow and haven't connected with before.*

Think about ways you can reach out to existing people. As well as trying to reduce your exposure to people who make you feel negative, try having a think about those in your life who lift you up and make you feel better about yourself. Is there a friend or colleague who, whenever you meet them, you leave brimming with confidence? This might not always be somebody obvious or even somebody who you are constantly in touch with, so if this is the case, think about ways that you could build on the relationship and try to see them more often. My grandma always told me that I should fill my time with people who are 'radiators, not drains', and it is advice that I have always tried to follow.

> *First Kaizen step: if you are feeling particularly low, try asking one of your friends to send you a daily compliment by text message. (Or if you suspect that a friend is feeling down, how about compiling several compliments from those around him/her and sending them?)*

Build some links with your local community. The fact that we now move accommodation a lot more than previous generations and often commute long distances to our jobs means that we feel less of a connection to the place that we live. This can be especially true if you live in a big city where the population is larger and more transient. If you are feeling this sense of disconnection, think of some small ways you can rebuild your links with your community. Can you volunteer or find a local class to join? If you have a baby or small children, are there fellow parents who you can try to connect with?

PRACTISING SELF-LOVE

Self-love sounds like something a crusty old hippy might start evangelizing about on a beach in Goa, BUT it is actually a great way to help combat your inner critic. Self-love or self-compassion is part of Buddhist teachings, which encourage showing patience, kindness and a non-judgemental attitude towards yourself. It is about accepting that you aren't always perfect, and acknowledging that there is always room for growth. As well as opening up to those around you, here are ideas for some small things to try to help you pick yourself up when you're feeling low:

Check in with yourself. If you are feeling particularly down on yourself, try closing your eyes for five minutes and doing a body scan. Identify areas of tension and then try taking a deep breath and breathing into them. Try relaxing your tongue and jaw, as this is usually an area that holds tension.

> *Kaizen First step: try the body-scan exercise on page 116.*

Practise self-massage. If there are areas of tension in your body, try gently massaging them to see if you can release any tight muscles. Most people can't afford a professional massage every day, sadly, but you will find that a lot can be done with a humble tennis ball! There are lots of online tutorials for how to practise this.

Use mindfulness to help treat your inner critic with compassion. If you find that you are overwhelmed with negative thoughts and your inner critic is running away with itself, take five minutes out to meditate (full guidelines on how to do so are on page 133). Let the negative thoughts pass over you and acknowledge that they exist, but try not to judge yourself. Note how you feel afterwards.

Treat your body like a friend. Rather than feeling like you are battling against your body, try thinking of it as a friend who you have to look after and who supports you. When you think bad thoughts about your body, stop yourself and question whether you would think something like that about a friend.

> *First Kaizen step: allocate one day to combat every bad thought you have with a positive thought.*

Be kind to yourself. Recall a time when a loved one or colleague has shown you kindness and think about how that felt. Perhaps write it down. Can you replicate that feeling when thinking about yourself?

Don't beat yourself up. If you have messed up at work or in a personal relationship, remember that everybody makes mistakes and that it is an experience that you can learn from. If you need to apologize to somebody then do so, then try not to punish yourself further.

Write down reminders of times when you felt good about yourself. Buy a pack of sticky notes and each morning write down a memory of when you felt good about yourself or proud of achieving something, such as 'The time when I helped the old man next door with his groceries' or 'The time when I looked completely amazing at Suze's wedding'.

> *First Kaizen step:* write a positive memory on a sticky note and attach it to your bedroom mirror to remind yourself of it all week.

Keep a compliment list or journal. As well as cultivating memories of when you felt good about yourself, remember to relish times when others have boosted you, too. If you receive a compliment from a friend, family member or colleague, write it down in your journal at the end of the day, or keep a list in the notes section of your phone. Return to the list whenever you feel a bit low and see if it transforms your mood.

Learn to say 'no' and set boundaries. Part of practising self-compassion is not over-stretching yourself by doing things that you don't want to do. Do you find that you are overwhelmed with trying to see everybody and fit everything in? Try to designate at least one or two nights per week for vegging out, doing your washing and cooking something healthy. Having more control over your own schedule and setting boundaries can feel wondrously liberating.

Set yourself a new challenge. If your confidence is low, learning a new skill or meeting new people can be a brilliant antidote. There are lots of ideas for how to go about this in the next chapter. Remember that it isn't about being perfect but about having fun and opening yourself up to new ways of enjoying yourself and/or new groups of people.

習慣化

shūkanka :
habits & challenges

● ● ● ● ● ● ● ○

HABITS & CHALLENGES | SHŪKANKA

*Great things are done by a series of small things
brought together* – Vincent Van Gogh

Up to this point, we have very much been concentrating on ways in which you can amend and improve your existing habits. The focus has been on interrogating the things that aren't working for you and making very small adjustments to your environment and how you go about your daily life. But acquiring entirely new habits and taking on exciting challenges can often be just as difficult to stick to as letting go of bad habits. You can start off full of inspiration about how you are going to become a cello virtuoso/caricaturist/tightrope walker/karate champion/expert baker (delete as appropriate) in the next year, but then find that other, seemingly more important, things get in the way or your motivation wavers. Using Kaizen techniques to introduce these new hobbies or challenges into your life at a gradual pace, with minimal disruption, can mean that you are more likely to keep up working towards your goal.

Acquiring a new hobby is great because it encourages you to learn new skills and adopt new habits. And, coming back to the Kaizen concept of *yokoten*, as you overcome the challenges and difficulties in your new hobby, you will build confidence, which will then build your confidence in other areas of your life and encourage you to

take on more challenges there too. Not only this, but getting a new hobby can be a great way to meet people who you have something in common with or provide some much-needed alone time away from children/work/housemates. When you are overwhelmed with the demands of daily life, hobbies can be a brilliant way to de-stress and refocus your mind. They stimulate your brain in a different way – a world away from work where you are answering endless emails, or spending your evening mindlessly scrolling through social media. It doesn't have to cost a fortune and doesn't involve doing anything that is detrimental to your health. What's not to like?!

It may be that you already have a strong passion for something and a keen idea of what you would like to take on as a new hobby. Or it could be that you know that you want to take on a new activity but haven't got much inspiration or a clue where to start. As children we are encouraged to adopt all sorts of hobbies and to challenge ourselves in new ways, but as an adult it can be hard to know where to start and how to find the time. In this section I'm going to provide some inspiration for various new activities you could try, along with advice on how to go about introducing these activities gradually into your routine, using Kaizen techniques, so that you are aware of what benefits they are bringing to your life and you are more likely to keep motivated to do them.

HOW TO CHOOSE A HOBBY

Rather than picking one hobby and spending lots of money on equipment or a whole package of lessons, first try out a few different things to see what you enjoy doing. Lots of courses or workshops will let you have a free 'taster' session, or ask your friend if you can try out the activity using their equipment. Trying out several

hobbies for size before committing will make you more likely
to pick one that will genuinely relax you and enhance your life.
Consider the following when choosing a new hobby:

Why do you want to do it in the first place? Consider the reasons
why you want to take up a new hobby. Is it because you want to get
outside more? Or spend more time away from work? To meet other
people in your area? Or simply to test yourself?

What were your childhood passions? Sometimes the hobbies that
you had as a child are things that you are genuinely interested in.
I used to play the piano and violin right up until I left school but
then let both things fall by the wayside when I went to university
and didn't have anywhere to practise. I'm determined to start
playing again soon. Think if you have similar childhood hobbies
that you could pick up again.

> *First Kaizen step: write down five things that you loved to do as a child and see if any might be worth picking up again.*

Do you have any neglected hobbies? As well looking at your childhood, are there any hobbies from your near-past that you could pick up again? Is there a half-written short story lying in a drawer or a fancy camera stored under your bed that you bought with the intention of getting into photography?

Get some inspiration! There are lots of ideas in the next section for small ways in which you can start to explore new hobbies and there are sources of inspiration all around too.

> *First Kaizen step: visit a bookshop, an art-supply shop, a sports shop or music shop, and note what you are most drawn towards. Do you automatically go to the cookbook section, to the crochet materials, or are you intrigued by all of the yoga equipment?*

Can you make it? Think about items that you regularly buy that you could make instead. Rather than spending lots of money on a new armchair, can you learn how to reupholster your existing chair? Can you make your own candles or knit your friend a scarf for his birthday rather than buy a new one?

Will this activity relax you? Whatever you choose for your hobbies, they should enhance your day and not feel like a drain. Be honest with yourself about what your skills are and what makes you happy, and you will be more likely to stick to the new hobby. If you love singing but are worried about your aptitude, join a choir that accepts all levels. If you don't have a natural aptitude for learning new languages, then taking that expensive Advanced Mandarin class is probably going to be a waste of money and energy, but starting a Beginner Mandarin very slowly in a Kaizen manner will be far less stressful. Similarly, if something bores you and doesn't excite you then it isn't worth committing time to either. Just because your friend has become an expert knitter of woodland animals doesn't mean you have to too. Your new hobby should be stress-free and fun, not a boring drain on your time!

Each person is different and will want to pursue their hobbies for varying reasons, so don't feel pressured to start an activity if you won't genuinely enjoy it. Think about what you want to get out of starting a new hobby. It might be that you like solving problems and so want a hobby that scratches that itch. It might be that you are having a stressful time of it and want an activity you can get lost in. It might be that you've moved to a new place and want a way to meet new people. Or it might be that you have a desire to improve your knowledge of something to stimulate your brain.

HOW TO STICK TO YOUR HOBBY

One of the main problems I have with trying out something new or resurrecting an old passion is that I start off full of enthusiasm which then wanes after a few weeks. I decide that I'm definitely going to write an award-winning feminist novel but then stop after a couple of writing sessions, or I buy a sketchbook so that my hidden artistic talents can finally rise to the surface and then never use it. I find it hard to fit new activities into my routine when I'm working, and often get frustrated that I'm not completely brilliant at something straight away. If you feel similarly, here are some tips for how to stick to your new hobby.

Start off very small. Remembering the Kaizen approach and introducing a new activity into your routine with the least amount of disruption will mean you are more likely to stick to it. It can help to peg the activity to something you already do. Start knitting while you watch the evening news every day, or use the ten minutes waiting for your morning coffee to brew to write one hundred words of your novel. When you get home from work, dedicate ten minutes to practising the piano before you do anything else.

Commit to spending time on your hobby. Rather than trying to fit in your new activity when you have a small break from all of your other commitments, allocate some set time to your new hobby. Fill out the time in your calendar and set a reminder so that you definitely don't plan anything else in its place.

Start your new activity at a time when you are more likely to stick to it. If you know that you are going to have a busy work period, then decide to take up the new hobby once that is over. Also, think carefully about the time of year and whether that will affect your motivation for doing something. For example, you may feel more inclined to take up indoorsy craft activities if it is cold and miserable outside, or you may be more likely to stick to your new birdwatching hobby when it is warm and sunny.

> *First Kaizen step: write down one hobby that you could start for each season of the year.*

Keep a reminder of why you have taken up the hobby in the first place. Hopefully, the fact that you have thought carefully about the hobby or challenge that you want to take up will mean that your passion will keep you motivated – at least initially. If you feel your motivation starting to wane, then it is helpful to have a reminder of why you wanted to do it in the first place.

> *First Kaizen step: stick a reminder of why you embarked on the activity in the first place to your mirror or kitchen fridge to keep you motivated.*

Ask friends and family to help. Involving your friends and family with your new hobby – whether that's showing them the drawings you've been doing or playing them the Bob Dylan song you have learned on the guitar – will help to positively reinforce your reasons for doing the activity in the first place. If you are worried that you might lose motivation, then ask them to keep checking up on you and hold you to account if you are working towards a particular goal.

Keep a record of how you are progressing and note the benefits of your new activity. If you are keeping a journal (see page 55), then dedicate a page of it to your new activity and write down each day if you have done something towards it and how it is making you feel.

Don't be too hard on yourself if you miss a few sessions. Life can sometimes get in the way of the goals that you have set so don't be harsh on yourself if your motivation wanes for a bit. The main thing is that you pick the activity back up.

BUT: don't plough on with something for the sake of it if you aren't enjoying it. If you really aren't finding your chosen new activity fun or relaxing, then it is far better to channel your energy into searching for a more stimulating hobby that you might have more chance of sticking to.

NEW CHALLENGES

I decided to learn Japanese and then move to Tokyo because I felt in need of a challenge and that my life could benefit from a shake-up. And being in Japan spurred me on to write this book, something that I would never have thought to do or committed the time to do beforehand. Your new challenges don't have to be quite as drastic as mine though, don't worry! Getting out of your comfort zone and testing yourself, whether that is becoming a master of sudoku puzzles or finally perfecting your illustration skills, can boost self-esteem, get you out of a rut, and give you new skills to employ in other areas of your life, such as your career. For anybody who really doesn't have any idea of what activity they would like to take up, here are some ideas for things you can try and small Kaizen-method-approved challenges to get started.

WORDS AND LANGUAGE

Commit to a writing challenge. Rather than sitting at your computer with a blank page in front of you, trying to magically be blessed with inspiration, try to do a small writing challenge each day instead. This can be the springboard for a bigger writing project and will get you in the habit of putting words down on the page. There are lots of podcasts and blogs dedicated to writing challenges.

Learn a new word every day. The OED and various other online services will email you a word and its etymology each day. Or seek one out yourself by looking in the dictionary.

> *First Kaizen step:* Start keeping a log of all of the new words that you discover – the more obscure, the better.

Improve your handwriting. If, like me, you feel like your handwriting has turned into a spidery mess now that you mostly use a computer to write, try out some calligraphy activities or take a course. My friend did a course before her wedding and saved a fortune on invitations and place cards, as she made her own with her beautiful handwriting.

Start a blog. There are now tonnes of online sites that will help you to put together a blog page for free. You can dedicate it to one of your passions or use it for a brain dump. Try to write an entry every day, even if it is just something very short. It can be for your personal consumption or a way to connect with friends or people who have similar interests. My boyfriend wrote a blog while we were in Japan and it was a great way of keeping in touch with people at home, updating them on what we had been up to, and keeping a catalogue of our many memories.

Start reading more. If you haven't read a book in ages, borrow one from the library or ask for a recommendation from a friend and dedicate a short amount of time each day to reading it – perhaps on your commute or just before you go to bed. Do you appreciate having some time away from a screen and a chance to be absorbed in another world or another person's voice? If you are already a regular reader, can you set yourself a challenge to read a certain number of books in a year or books only written by authors from different countries?

> *First Kaizen step:* *find a new book and try to read it within a fortnight.*

Improve your general knowledge. It could be that you want to do better on the pub quiz machine or complete crosswords faster. Or that you feel like your knowledge of Manchester United's 1992 squad is lacking or that you wish you knew more about the French Revolution. Try choosing one topic a week to learn about and then read some online articles, listen to TEDx talks or podcasts, or open a good old-fashioned book about it. Over the course of the day, make a note of any other topics you come across that you would like to know some more about, whether that's something you read online, in a newspaper or something you heard about at work.

> **First Kaizen step:** *listen to a TEDx talk or informative podcast and then tell a friend or partner about what you have learned.*

Start learning a language online. Is there a language that you started learning at school but which you let fall by the wayside? Or are you planning to visit a new country and want to know some of the language before you get there? It is never too late to learn another language, and one of the great benefits of all the technology that we now have access to is that it has made it very cheap and accessible to do so. There are lots of language-learning apps that you can download onto your phone or online courses that you can take. If you are unsure which language you would like to try, testing some out on your language-learning app can be a great way to see if you get on with it before you commit. I learned Japanese for six months before my trip to Japan, and practising the various characters on a flashcard app on my phone really helped me to learn the three alphabets more quickly.

> **First Kaizen step:** *download a language-learning app and try it out for thirty minutes.*

Or learn a language IRL. If you have tried out a few different languages for size and decided that you want to take it to the next level, then why not sign up to a course? I used to find that my weekly Japanese lesson after work was a great way to switch my brain to doing something that wasn't just answering emails. If you don't have the means to fork out for a language course then social media can be a great way to connect with others who might be wishing to learn a language – my friend learns French by having conversational lessons with a French guy she met via Twitter, and in turn, he learns English from her. All for free! Having a partner or friend to practise with can keep you both motivated too.

SOUNDS

Educate yourself about a new musical genre. Have you always wished that you knew more about classical music? Or the history of rock 'n' roll? There are infinite online resources for learning about music, whether that is falling down a YouTube hole of watching lots of music videos, or seeking out documentaries. I always feel ashamed that I don't know enough about classical music so have started to listen to classical-music radio stations when I have a task to complete at work and need music to help me concentrate and block out the rest of the office.

Learn an instrument. Have you always wanted to master Joni Mitchell on the guitar to impress your friends at dinner parties? Or play jazz piano in a smoky low-lit nightclub to a crowd of glamorous people on dinner dates? Or did you learn the clarinet at school but desert it as soon as you started to fancy boys instead?! Taking up an instrument as an adult can be a really rewarding experience and a great hobby to help you decompress after a stressful day at work. You don't have to commit to expensive lessons and buying a brand-new instrument from the very start. Buy a cheap second-hand instrument, try one out in a music shop or music library or borrow one from a friend to see if you like it. There are also hundreds of online video tutorials and courses for you to explore before taking the plunge with proper lessons. Starting small and inexpensive to see if it is a hobby that fits with your routine will mean you have more chance of persevering rather than blowing a load of money on an expensive instrument, practising for a few days and then letting it sit under your bed for the rest of eternity.

Improve your singing voice. Whether you are a budding soprano who has never reached the heights of success that you deserve, or a tone-deaf karaoke fiend who wants to be able to do a better rendition of Lady Gaga, there is always room for improvement. Seek out the hundreds of online videos about singing technique and practise, practise, practise!

ART AND CRAFTS

Start making your own clothes and accessories. Whether you prefer to sew, knit or crochet, learning how to make your own clothes can be immensely satisfying – and can save or make you lots of money, too. Start off with a very small project, such as knitting a scarf for a baby or sewing together a cushion cover or tote bag, and see how you go from there. Cheap offcuts of material can often be found in charity shops, on sale at craft stores or online on second-hand sites. Patterns can often be found for free or very cheaply online, or club together with a friend to buy them and share.

Get into flower arranging. Kado, or the art of flower arranging, is a very popular activity in Japan, and there are over 2,000 schools dedicated to teaching the subject. While flower arrangement in the West consists of symmetrically arranging flowers in a vase, Japanese Ikebana (literally 'flowers kept alive') involves far more complex arrangements; there are different styles of arrangement depending on the school and the plants and vase used. The emphasis is not just on the flowers themselves, but on the whole arrangement and how all of the various elements work in harmony with each other. Find a local flower-arranging course or learn via the plentiful online resources available. Your local florist will also be a useful source of information – and will potentially give you some leftover flowers and extras too.

Brush up on your art history. Would you love to know some more about Hokusai's wave paintings? Or Picasso's Blue Period? There are now lots of ways to learn about art that don't have to involve committing to an expensive art history degree.

> *First Kaizen step: pick one artist and look up one of their paintings every day for a week. Or read something about an art movement for five minutes each day.*

Start drawing and/or painting. Did you enjoy art classes at school, like me, but haven't picked up a pencil or paintbrush since? When you're younger, sitting down and drawing or colouring is second nature, however good you are at it, but as you get older the habit often falls by the wayside, especially if you feel like you don't have a talent for it. Being creative has been shown to increase dopamine (the pleasure hormone) levels, and art therapy is regularly used as a way to treat a number of conditions, including depression and anxiety, as it reduces stress levels and increases self-esteem, and it also improves memory retention.[34]

> *First Kaizen step: try spending five minutes of your day drawing somebody – whether that is your husband or a stranger – and see how you feel afterwards.*

Make cards and presents. Rather than forking out for expensive birthday cards or thank-you notes, can you be creative and make them yourself? If you feel like your painting or drawing skills need work, then can you make a collage of photos that mean something to your recipient? I'm sure it will be more treasured than a random shop-bought card and will be much cheaper too. Similarly, rather than spending a small fortune on a wedding present that your friends will forget about, can you make them a print of a poem or song that means something to them?

FOOD

Learn to make your favourite takeaway meal from scratch. If
you aren't a very confident cook or are looking to save some
money, challenge yourself to make your favourite dish from
scratch. Teaching yourself some basic skills and favourite flavour
combinations can revolutionize your attitude to cooking. There are
lots of resources to help, either online or in cookery books, and you
could enlist the assistance of your partner/friends/family too.

Try out a cookery technique you have never tried before. If you are
already a capable cook, think of a recipe or cookery technique that
you have never made before and try it out, whether that is making a
soufflé that doesn't immediately sink or the perfect pad thai.

Broaden your horizons. Seek out a cuisine that you have never tried
before and research the food culture. There are hundreds of brilliant
food documentaries on streaming services now. If you are lucky
enough to live in a big city with a varied food culture, then try out
the new cuisine in real life, or otherwise try to make a dish at home.

Start a supper or cake club. If you feel like your culinary talents are
ready to be shown to the world, turn your hobby into something
you can share with your friends or colleagues. My friend has a
monthly 'pie club' with her friends where each month a different
member of the group makes a pie and they all meet up to eat it. Not
only do they get to sample a delicious pie each month, but it's an
ideal excuse to regularly see each other when their schedules are

all so busy. If you are a baker, then a cake club at work can be the perfect way to bond with new colleagues and show off your skills. You could even sell your items and donate the money to a different charity each month.

THE OUTDOORS

Get to know the history of the area in which you live. Do you live in a town or city but have little knowledge of the local history? Do you know the story behind the old factory building that has now been turned into luxury flats? Have you noticed any unusual architecture? When I visit a new place, I love exploring on foot and finding out about the history around me, but I rarely do so when I'm home and in the places where I spend most of my time. Local libraries can be a great source of information on the history of your area, or see if there are any walking tours available. And if you are in a city with lots of tall buildings, remember to look up – you often see a whole other side to a place above ground.

Get out further afield. Is there a part of your city or a town nearby which you have never visited even though you have always meant to?

> *First Kaizen step: if you have a bike, then try cycling just a bit further away from your usual route and exploring a new place. Or catch local transport to a station or stop which you have never been to before. You might be pleasantly surprised by what you find.*

Learn about nature. When I was little, I was always curious about what a leaf/plant/tree/bird I had just spotted was, but this curiosity disappeared when I was at school and there was so much more information to cram into my brain. But I am finding that as I get older, this desire to know more about nature and the environment is returning. I live in south London where there are hundreds of parakeets living in my local park – something you'd never expect in such a big city (and, amazingly, people still aren't absolutely sure how they got here). I find myself constantly surprised by the variety of nature that manages to survive in spite of all of the pollution and noise. But I still wish that I could automatically identify a species of bird or tree or flower just by looking at it. If you feel the same, how about challenging yourself to learn about one of these topics? Aside from the plentiful amount of books on the subject, there are now some really useful identification apps that you can download too.

Try out shinrin-yoku, or Japanese forest bathing. Getting out in nature has been shown to have multiple benefits for both our mental and physical health. A guide to the art of Japanese forest bathing can be found on page 252. Not only is it easy to do by yourself or with a partner/friend but there are now *shinrin-yoku* groups starting up around the world, if you are keen to hang out with fellow forest bathers in your area.

THE ART OF *SHINRIN-YOKU,* OR JAPANESE FOREST BATHING

Shinrin- (forest) *yoku* (bathing) became popular in Japan in the 1980s as a form of nature therapy for its stressed-out and overworked citizens, after the government conducted a series of studies into the benefits of getting out into nature. The idea was to go and immerse yourself in designated forest areas in order to rejuvenate your mind. It was a way to get people outside and encourage healthier lifestyles, and eventually it became properly introduced as a public health programme. The Shinto religion in Japan puts much emphasis on the importance of nature, and the Japanese have honoured sacred spirits in nature – in mountains, rocks, rivers and trees – since ancient times. This, coupled with the abundance of forest areas in the mountainous archipelago that is Japan, means it is no real surprise that forest bathing originated there. But the good news is that you can practise forest bathing in any green space that you can find; it doesn't have to involve a lengthy car journey to find the perfect pine forest. And, despite the name, no actual bathing in water is required!

THE BENEFITS OF *SHINRIN-YOKU*

A number of studies have shown the health benefits of *shinrin-yoku*.[35] Spending just two hours immersed in nature can boost our immunity, lower blood pressure, balance the nervous and parasympathetic systems, reduce stress levels and increase cognitive function. It can be highly beneficial to our mental health and help to combat Seasonal Affective Disorder (SAD). And the health benefits of being in nature have been shown to be more pronounced than a walk for a similar amount of time in a busy city environment.

HOW TO FOREST BATHE

So where do you start? Here are some tips for how to go about your first forest bathing experience:

Find a green space. It will ideally be a forest or a wood, but any sort of large green space will work. You can always use it as an excuse to try out a new area you have never explored before.

Be prepared. It won't be very fun to wander around a forest if it is dark or wet, so check the weather forecast beforehand. Take enough food and water, wear appropriate footwear, and bring a map if there is a chance that you might get lost.

Turn your phone off. This should be a mindful experience without distractions, so turn your phone off or put it on to airplane mode.

Don't see it as exercise. The emphasis is on fully immersing yourself in nature and appreciating it, not on going for a vigorous workout. Start to explore the area really slowly on foot and take it all in. Take your time and be chill.

Don't have an end point. Rather than sticking to a set route with an end point, walk wherever the mood takes you and be present (although take a map so that you don't get hopelessly lost!). The idea is to savour the feeling of being in nature, not to try to accomplish anything else.

Breathe. If it won't embarrass you too much(!), find a quiet spot to close your eyes and just breathe in and out. Pay attention to your breath and then start to deepen it. Relax your shoulders and release any tension that you are carrying. Keep going until you feel that your breath has regulated itself into a regular slow rhythm.

Be mindful. Take in what you can see around you. Look up and around. What smells hit you? What sounds can you hear? Is it hot/cold? Can you feel a breeze? Touch some nearby leaves or a tree trunk to see what they feel like. If there is a stream, then dip your hands or feet in the water. Appreciate the green around you and the absence of pollution/sirens/angry people.

Take your time and reflect. Spend as much time as you like wandering around and taking in your surroundings. Think of how little time you ever spend just being in nature and free of annoying distractions. If you are finding it hard to relax and are itching to look at your phone, note that feeling and reflect on it.

Once you have finished your *shinrin-yoku* session note how you feel. Are you more relaxed than when you started? Did you find it easy or hard to completely switch off? Did you miss your devices? If you feel invigorated by the experience, then try doing it again and see if you manage to switch off a bit more each time. It can be something that you do entirely alone or you can involve your partner, friends or kids. See if you can get them to fall in love with nature too!

Beginning is easy, continuing is hard – Japanese proverb

stumbling blocks

● ● ● ● ● ● ●

STUMBLING BLOCKS

Your experience of Kaizen is unlikely to be a linear one. Everybody starts off very motivated to try new habits or get rid of unhealthy ones and then struggles to keep it up when other priorities get in the way. It can be especially hard to persevere when life throws a curveball, such as a job loss, a relationship breakdown, a bereavement or a health scare. When something shocking or stressful happens, it can be easy to slip back into the comfort of old behaviours and not look after yourself properly. Similarly, if your environment changes in a dramatic way, such as a big house move, a job change, retirement or the arrival of a new baby, it can make you crave routine, even if it's one that isn't very good for you.

Kaizen is a lifelong commitment to change, so there may be times when your motivation wavers or when you fall on hard times (unless you're the luckiest person in the world). Nobody is perfect, and the idea isn't to achieve complete perfection. It's about approaching life as an exciting journey and opportunity for improvement. Bringing it back to Toyota's car production line where this all started, it is about developing new ideas and practices while also polishing and refining your existing methods. There will be inevitable stumbling blocks along the way, but there are some methods to keep in mind to make sure you continue with Kaizen.

Plan for setbacks. Before embarking upon a new activity or planning to give up a bad habit, think about some of the things that might trip you up along the way. If you are trying to cut down on your alcohol consumption, then be mindful of an upcoming holiday with your friends where you might feel pressured into drinking a lot. Or if you are planning to run a marathon in spring, think about how the bad weather in winter might affect your motivation to train. Being mindful of potential stumbling blocks will help you to approach them in a different way if they do occur.

Choose the activity to suit the time of year. If it is cold and dark outside, you will feel far less inclined to finally start outdoor swimming than if you tried it during warm weather. Think carefully about when you are most likely to keep up a new habit, and plan accordingly. Just because everybody else is trying a new extreme exercise routine in January doesn't mean that you have to!

Celebrate your successes. Keeping track of your progress and noting the different milestones you have completed will help you to keep going if your motivation starts to waver. Success breeds success, so completing one challenge will then spur you on to try something else. For example, if you create a nice living space at home and start enjoying it, then you might feel more inclined to create a nice working space, too.

Get some cheerleaders. Involving your friends, colleagues and family in your Kaizen goals means that there will be more people to encourage you and support you if you are finding things tough. They can also help to remove temptations that might set you back, perhaps inviting you for a coffee instead of wine if you are trying to cut down on booze, or buying fruit for the office snack supply rather than cakes.

Go back to small. If you are finding that you are struggling to keep to your targets, reduce them to the very smallest possible thing you can do instead. If you are having a bad mental health day and don't feel capable of going for a 5K run, then try to go for a small walk instead. Even just doing something small is better than nothing, and you can gradually work your way back up to your target again.

Difficult times can teach you a lot about yourself. Although suffering a job loss, a relationship breakdown or a bereavement can be utterly

devastating and make you feel like the rug has been completely pulled out from underneath you, they can also be the times when you learn a lot about yourself and your resilience. Be proud of yourself for making it through the day and what you have achieved, however small. The Japanese and Chinese alphabets don't have a single symbol for the word 'crisis'. Instead, it is an amalgamation of the two symbols for 'danger' (危) and 'good opportunity' (機). It is hard to see the wood through the trees when you are having a hard time, but remembering that good things can come out of adversity can be helpful. All of my relationship break-ups have led to more satisfactory relationships in the future, and the time I got made redundant from my job actually led to me getting a far better job a few weeks later, so try to keep in mind that good things, as well as bad, can be round the corner.

> *First Kaizen step: if you're having a tough time, keep a record of one small thing that you have achieved each day, then look back on this when things are feeling better and congratulate yourself on your resilience and for getting through.*

And the most important thing: don't be hard on yourself. If you are already having a rough time of it, then beating yourself up for not hitting your goals will only make you feel far worse. Be kind to yourself and remember that you can return to your new habits or activities whenever you are feeling stronger. Start small and build it up again.

CONCLUSION

CHANGE FOR GOOD

Although we have reached the end of the book, I hope that this is just the beginning of your Kaizen practice. You should now have an overview of the ideas behind Kaizen and a good understanding of the theory of constant improvement, along with some inspiration for ways in which you can go about acquiring new skills, develop productive habits and let go of some of the bad ones. And remember that Kaizen is not one-size-fits-all; one person's experience of it will be entirely different from another's. The important thing is to listen to your mind and body, then create good habits that work for you and let go of the ones that aren't doing you any favours. Making small improvements in one area will then inspire you with the confidence to go out and achieve improvement in another.

The emphasis is on *continuous* improvement, so you should always be thinking about ways you can be tweaking your routine or simplifying your life. Staying mindful of your feelings and behaviours will mean that you will be more aware of when you need to take a step back or if you need a new challenge to get you out of a rut. Before I went away, I had the worst FOMO and used to say 'yes' to absolutely every invitation, even if I was already knackered and/ or broke. This meant that I had a very active social life but my sleep, anxiety levels and bank balance were suffering as a result. Although it was hard to be away from my friends while I was in Japan, it did teach me two important lessons: that they were still there when I returned and that it's always better to decline an invitation and look after yourself than to try to stretch yourself in too many directions.

It is about managing your limited physical and mental energy to ensure that you aren't burnt out. It will make you a better partner/friend/colleague/family member and you'll be more prepared to face the challenges of the outside world.

We live in a culture that expects immediate results and that rewards overnight success, so it is no surprise that a lot of our self-help and health trends also promote quick wins and miracle cures. There is so much noise and misinformation surrounding us that it can be easy to forget to listen to your mind and body and to go with what works for you. This why Kaizen is so effective. Tracking your habits, stepping out of your regular routines, and analysing your feelings will mean that you tailor new habits and tweak old ones to make sure that they work for you. Working towards your goal at a steady pace without having to commit lots of time, energy or money towards it will also mean that you aren't taking on a lot of risk. You can try out new routines for size and then adjust them if they aren't working. And the whole process will result in you knowing yourself better; you will understand why you react to situations in a certain way and have more of an idea about where your strengths and weaknesses lie.

And remember to keep looking back on what you have achieved and to regularly reward yourself too. If you have been keeping a gratitude journal, then return to it often to see what and who has helped you along the way. See change as an ongoing process. If some of your new habits fall by the wayside, then don't beat yourself up. Think about how you can pick your good habits back up in very small increments and how you can eliminate some of the obstacles that got in your way the first time.

If you are finding that Kaizen is working for you and transforming your habits, then one good thing you can do is to encourage others to take up Kaizen too. Whether that is supporting people you know in your own life to achieve something new or finding others online who are looking to embark upon a similar challenge. Connecting with others and sharing advice will also allow you to reflect on what you have achieved and perhaps give you fresh inspiration for new ways in which you can change.

ABOUT THE AUTHOR

Sarah Harvey was living in Tokyo working as a freelance book scout and publishing consultant when she fell in love with Japanese culture and was introduced to Kaizen. After a life-changing time away, Sarah now lives in London, where she works for a literary agency and spends a not-insignificant portion of her time searching for a Japanese-standard bowl of Tonkotsu ramen.

ACKNOWLEDGEMENTS

First of all I want to thank the brilliant team at Bluebird. Particular shout outs to Martha Burley, Hockley Raven Spare, and Zainab Dawood, who have carved my words into much better shape and made this process so easy. Thank you also to my copy editor Laura Herring for her excellent improvements, to Rachel Graves for the Kanji openers, and to Justine Anweiler and Mel Four for the incredible design, illustrations, and cover. I also want to thank my Rights Queens and fellow Nando's/karaoke enthusiasts Anna Shora and Emma Winter, who have done such a stellar job selling Kaizen around the world. Also thanks to Jon Mitchell for taking me Stateside – unlike Take That, I will break America! And finally, thank you to my publisher Carole Tonkinson for being such a great champion and for having faith that I could do this from the beginning.

I also want to say thanks to Ben Gardner for his illuminating insights on habitual behaviour, to Euclides A. Coimbra at the Kaizen Institute for his assistance with understanding the Kaizen method, and to Keiko Todo for casting a keen second eye over the Japanese references.

To Lizzie Ackerman, the Paul Chuckle to my Barry Chuckle (R.I.P.): thank you for always having my (piggy) back, making me laugh every day, and for visiting me in Japan for what was an unforgettable time. I hope some of the tidying tips will be of use to you. To Mary Doherty, who was always there to make me a calming ginger tea when I was fretting about my word count and for generally being the toppest of babes: THANK YOU. And sending lots of love to the rest of my Lovely Ladies: Kate Blatchford, Dani Salamon, Jen Kenwood, and Rachael Henry. You managed to avoid me in Manchester but you've got me for life now. Sorry about that.

To my oldest and dearest friends: Kath Preston, Rav Virdi, Jess Barnett, Becky Donnelly, Jenny Baker, and Suzie Moore. I hope we have many more weekends of sitting in our pants, watching true crime, and not having showers. It is very rare to still be friends with people you met two decades ago, when we had weird mullet hairdos (actually, that was just me) and a penchant for sub-standard indie bands (that was all of us), but we're still going! Here's to many more decades.

Thank you also to Sam Hutchinson for his endless amounts of sage advice and for just being a top pal in general.

Before I run out of superlatives and this gets a bit too 'Gwyneth Paltrow at the Oscars', I want to say a final thank you to my family. To my parents Josie and Brendon for their unwavering love and support and for making the trip to come and see me on my travels; I will never forget it. To Will Harvey and Lea Marsden, whose steady supply of football memes and supportive messages have kept me going whilst writing this. I'm so lucky to have you guys. And to fellow ramen enthusiast Lucy Pritchett for being my Sista from Another Mista and for always helping me put the world to rights. Finally, to my partner-in-crime Joe Mosby, without who this adventure would never have happened. Thank you for talking me down off several ledges during this process and just always being my biggest fan.

ENDNOTES

1   *Japan Times*. www.japantimes.co.jp/
    news/2017/11/02/national/social-
    issues/japan-drops-114th-gender-
    equality-rankings-world-economic-
    forum/#.W46jOpNKjVo

2   BBC online. www.bbc.co.uk/news/
    business-39981997

3   Imai, Masaaki, *KAIZEN: The Key to
    Japan's Competitive Success*, (McGraw-
    Hill Publishing Company, New York,
    1986), p. 3.

4   A clear and concise introduction to
    the history of Kaizen can be found
    in Robert Maurer's book, *One Small
    Step Can Change Your Life* (Workman
    Publishing, New York, 2014),
    pp. 23–31. There is also an overview
    in Mr Imai's *KAIZEN*, pp. 10–13.

5   Maurer, Robert, *One Small Step*, pp.
    29–31.

6   Maurer, Robert, *One Small Step*, p. 30.

7   Imai, Masaaki, *KAIZEN*, p. 3.

8   More on Sir Dave Brailsford's
    management techniques can be found
    in his interview with *Harvard Business
    Review*: hbr.org/2015/10/how-1-
    performance-improvements-led-to-
    olympic-gold

9   Tate online. www.tate.org.uk/art/art-
    terms/j/japonisme

10 'The strength of habit'. Orbell, S., &
    Verplanken, B. (2015), *Health Psychology
    Review*, 9(3), 311–317.

11 'How are habits formed: Modelling
    habit formation in the real world,'

    Lally, P.; Van Jaarsveld, C.H.M.; Potts,
    H.W.W.; Wardle, J.; (2010) *EUR J SOC
    PSYCHOL*, 40 (6) 998–1009.

12 A good overview of negativity bias
    can be found in Dr Danny Penman's
    Mindfulness for Creativity (Piatkus,
    London, 2015) pp. 22–40.

13 *Independent*. www.independent.
    co.uk/life-style/quitters-day-new-
    years-resolutions-give-up-fail-
    today-a8155386.html

14 Robert Maurer, *The Spirit of Kaizen*,
    p. 18.

15 Imai, Masaaki, *KAIZEN*, p. 163.

16 A good introduction to this belief is
    in Velizara Chervenkova's *Japanese
    Psychotherapies: Silence and Body-Mind
    Interconnectedness* (Springer Nature,
    Singapore, 2017), pp. 37–40.

17 World Health Organization. www.
    who.int/dietphysicalactivity/factsheet_
    inactivity/en/

18 NHS online. www.nhs.uk/live-well/
    eat-well/water-drinks-nutrition/

19 University College London.
    www.ucl.ac.uk/news/news-
    articles/0414/010413-fruit-veg-
    consumption-death-risk

20 NHS online. www.nhs.uk/live-well/
    eat-well/how-to-cut-down-on-sugar-
    in-your-diet/

21 Sleep Foundation. sleepfoundation.
    org/excessivesleepiness/content/why-
    do-we-need-sleep

22 Reading Agency. readingagency.org. uk/adults/impact/research/reading-well-books-on-prescription-scheme-evidence-base.html

23 NHS online. www.nhs.uk/live-well/ eat-well/healthy-breakfasts-recipes/

24. www.psychologytoday.com/us/blog/ click-here-happiness/201802/how-break-your-phone

25 http://hdl.handle.net/2077/28893

26 Ruoxu Wang, Fan Yang, Michel M. Haigh, 'Let me take a selfie: Exploring the psychological effects of posting and viewing selfies and groupies on social media,' *Telematics and Informatics*, Volume 34, Issue 4, 2017, pp. 274–283, www.sciencedirect.com/ science/article/abs/pii/ S0736585315301350

27 Boubekri M., Cheung I.N., Reid K.J., Wang C.H., Zee P.C. 'Impact of windows and daylight exposure on overall health and sleep quality of office workers: a case-control pilot study'. *J Clin Sleep Med* 2014; 10(6): pp. 603–611

28 Nieuwenhuis, M., Knight, C., Postmes, T., & Haslam, S. A. (2014). 'The relative benefits of green versus lean office space: Three field experiments'. *Journal of Experimental Psychology: Applied, 20*(3), pp. 199–214.

29 Becker, William J.; Belkin, Liuba; Tuskey, Sarah, 'Killing me softly: Electronic communications monitoring and employee and spouse well-being,' *Academy of Management Proceedings*, VOL. 2018, NO. 1 journals.aom.org/ doi/pdf/10.5465/AMBPP.2018.121

30 Thorley C. (2017) 'Not By Degrees: Improving student mental health in the UK's Universities', IPPR. www.ippr.org/research/ publications/not-by-degrees

31 *Guardian* online. www.theguardian. com/cities/2017/nov/16/japan-reusa-ble-housing-revolution

32 www.ncbi.nlm.nih.gov/pmc/ articles/PMC4607089/

33 Saphire-Bernstein, S., & Taylor, S. (2013-01-01). 'Close Relationships and Happiness' *Oxford Handbook of Happiness*. (Oxford University Press). Retrieved 14 Oct. 2018, from www.oxfordhandbooks. com/view/10.1093/oxford-hb/9780199557257.001.0001 /oxfordhb-9780199557257-e-060.

34 www.ncbi.nlm.nih.gov/pmc/articles/ PMC4041074/

35 Li, Q., Morimoto, K., Nakadai, A., Inagaki, H., Katsumata, M., Shimi-zu, T., … Kawada, T. (2007). 'Forest Bathing Enhances Human Natural Killer Activity and Expression of Anti-Cancer Proteins'. *International Journal of Immunopathology and Pharmacology*, 3–8. https://doi. org/10.1177/03946320070200S202; Li, Q., Morimoto, K., Kobayashi, M., Inagaki, H., Katsumata, M., Hirata, Y., Krensky, A. M. (2008). 'Visiting a Forest, but Not a City, Increases Human Natural Killer Activity and Expression of Anti-Cancer Proteins'. *International Journal of Immunopathology and Pharmacology*, 117–127. doi. org/10.1177/039463200802100113

PICTURE CREDITS